A NEW MODEL OF SCHOOL DISCIPLINE

Engaging Students and Preventing Behavior Problems

David R. Dupper

OXFORD WORKSHOP SERIES

OXFORD
UNIVERSITY PRESS

2010

OXFORD
UNIVERSITY PRESS

Oxford University Press, Inc., publishes works that further
Oxford University's objective of excellence
in research, scholarship, and education.

Oxford   New York
Auckland   Cape Town   Dar es Salaam   Hong Kong   Karachi
Kuala Lumpur   Madrid   Melbourne   Mexico City   Nairobi
New Delhi   Shanghai   Taipei   Toronto

With offices in
Argentina   Austria   Brazil   Chile   Czech Republic   France   Greece
Guatemala   Hungary   Italy   Japan   Poland   Portugal   Singapore
South Korea   Switzerland   Thailand   Turkey   Ukraine   Vietnam

Published by Oxford University Press, Inc.
198 Madison Avenue, New York, New York 10016

www.oup.com

Library of Congress Cataloging-in-Publication Data
Dupper, David R.
A new model of school discipline : engaging students and preventing
behavior problems / David R. Dupper.
p.   cm. — (Oxford workshop series)
Includes bibliographical references and index.
ISBN 978-0-19-537807-8
1. School discipline—United States.   2. Rewards and punishments in
education—United States.   3. Problem children—United States.   I. Title.
LB3012.2.D86 2010
371.5—dc22
2009034606

1   3   5   7   9   8   6   4   2

Printed in the United States of America
on acid-free paper

A NEW MODEL OF SCHOOL DISCIPLINE

I dedicate this book to all the at-risk youth with whom I have worked over the years, and to all those current and future youth struggling through school with behavioral problems.

Contents

Preface

Current disciplinary practices in U.S. public schools are largely based on punishing and removing students from school. There has been a near epidemic of suspensions over the past decade for relatively minor or vaguely defined student offenses. Students of color and students from disadvantaged backgrounds are at an increased risk of being suspended. While there is little, if any, evidence to suggest that suspensions have increased school safety or improved student behavior, we do know that school suspension is a moderate to strong predictor of dropping out of school. Moreover, corporal punishment is legal today in 21 states, and it is used frequently in 13 states.

Current disciplinary policies and procedures in the vast majority of our schools are antithetical to social work values and a democratic society and harm a significant number of young people. We face a stark choice. We can continue to punish and exclude misbehaving students from our schools and add to the already high number of school failures and dropouts, or we can try a different approach. In this book, I contend that there is a pressing need to change the way that we think about school discipline and to question the adequacy of the current paradigm upon which our school discipline policies and practices have been built. In the following pages, I argue strongly that there is a need to move to a new model of school discipline that is proactive, preventive, and relationship based and that focuses on connecting students with schools rather than punishing and excluding them.

My intent is to provide social workers and other child advocates with cutting-edge research and best practices in alternatives to exclusionary and punitive disciplinary policies and practices in schools. This workshop book highlights and describes cutting-edge, state of the art programs and strategies that have been shown to improve school climates, prevent or reduce student behavior problems, increase students' connectedness with school, and contribute to and support a relationship-based, preventive model of school discipline. Perhaps most importantly, I discuss best practices to equip "change agents" with knowledge and skills needed to overcome barriers and increase the chances of success in implementing and sustaining effective programs and strategies.

In Chapter 1, I discuss a number of issues surrounding the most widely implemented school disciplinary practices in U.S. public schools today: out-of-school suspension and expulsion. I discuss the current prevalence of suspensions, the effectiveness of suspensions, and health and social problems that have been shown to be associated with suspensions. I also examine what we know about the reasons why students are suspended from school and raise a number of questions and concerns about the way in which certain categories of offenses are defined and reported. I also discuss issues surrounding the disproportionate rates of suspensions for African American and Hispanic students. The chapter concludes with a brief discussion of the prevalence and outcomes associated with the use of corporal punishment in those states where it remains legal.

In Chapter 2, I provide several disparate definitions of the word *discipline*, and I present a brief historical overview of several important forces that have shaped and continue to shape discipline in U.S. public schools. This chapter includes a discussion of the profound impact of Puritanism over several centuries, major Supreme Court cases and federal and state legislation since the 1960s, and the impact of Department of Education mandates and No Child Left Behind (NCLB) legislation. This chapter then moves to a discussion of a uniquely Western cultural phenomenon—the infantilization of our youth—and its impact on how we think about our youth and, in turn, how we discipline them. This chapter concludes by arguing that the current discipline paradigm in U.S. public schools is ineffective and harmful and that a new way of thinking about school discipline and the policies and practices that result from this new way of thinking are needed.

In Chapter 3, I describe a new school discipline paradigm that is comprehensive, preventive, and based on enhancing relationships. I argue that school discipline is a complex and interactive process involving a number of school contextual factors, and I discuss those factors that impact student behavior. I emphasize the importance of school connectedness in reducing discipline problems and highlight five school characteristics that are important in assessing the extent to which students feel "connected" to their school. This chapter concludes with a discussion of assumptions and central tenets of this new relationship-based, preventive model of school discipline.

In Chapter 4, I present a rationale for developing and implementing comprehensive, multitiered interventions to reduce behavior problems in schools, and I briefly catalog an array of empirically supported strategies and programs at each intervention level (i.e., primary/universal, secondary/

targeted, and tertiary/remedial) designed to meet the needs of students while also meeting the unique needs of an individual school district in the most effective, pragmatic, and cost-efficient manner possible. I also discuss widely used school security measures that have not been empirically supported in improving school climate or reducing student behavior problems. Finally, I make a series of recommendations for improving the ways in which school discipline data are collected and reported to the general public.

In Chapter 5, I discuss the hard part: making organizational changes in schools. I document the significant challenges to making school-wide organizational changes in general as well as the unique obstacles to changing school discipline practices. I draw from the works of several authors to present a five-stage strategic planning process designed to move from a traditional, punitive model of school discipline to a relationship-based model of discipline. This chapter concludes with several additional key points to consider in making significant systemic changes in schools.

My hope is that this book will motivate and equip social workers and other child advocates with the knowledge, skills, and tools necessary to bring about systemic change in current school discipline policies and practices. It is imperative that we carry out this increasingly important task by eliminating unproductive student behaviors, rather than the students themselves.

A NEW MODEL OF SCHOOL DISCIPLINE

1

■ ■ ■

Current Disciplinary Practices: An Overview

In this chapter, I discuss a number of issues surrounding two of the most widely implemented school disciplinary practices in U.S. public schools today: out-of-school suspension and expulsion. I discuss the current prevalence of suspensions, the effectiveness of suspensions, and health and social problems that have been shown to be associated with suspensions. I also examine what we know about the reasons why students are suspended from school, and I raise a number of questions and concerns about the way in which certain categories of offenses are defined and reported. I also discuss issues surrounding the disproportionate rates of suspensions for African American and Hispanic students. I conclude this chapter with a brief discussion of the prevalence and outcomes associated with the use of corporal punishment in those states where it remains legal.

An Epidemic of Suspensions?

Over the years, schools have typically responded to inappropriate student behaviors by referring the student to the principal's office, assigning detention, or assigning students to in-school suspension. However, schools are using out-of-school suspension and expulsion as disciplinary responses to student misbehavior much more frequently over the past decade, resulting in what some consider a near epidemic of out-of-school suspensions (Fenning & Bohanon, 2006; Rausch & Skiba, 2004; Richart, Brooks, & Soler, 2003). Data compiled by the National Center for Education Statistics appear to support such claims. Specifically, in 2002, U.S. public schools meted out 3.1 million suspensions, or 6.6% of the total number of students (Snyder, Dillow, & Hoffman, 2007) and 89,131 students or 0.2% of the total number of students were expelled (Snyder et al., 2007). In 2006, the number of students suspended and expelled increased to over 3.3 million students, which was 6.9% of the total number of students that year (Snyder, Dillow, & Hoffman, 2009).

Are Out-of-School Suspensions Effective?

Do out-of-school suspensions "work"? Are they effective? The answer largely depends on the desired outcome. If the desired outcome is to remove the offending student from school (American Academy of Pediatrics, 2003) and provide temporary relief to frustrated teachers and administrators (Bock, Tapscott, & Savner, 1998), out-of-school suspensions are unquestionably effective. However, it is also important to recognize that an out-of-school suspension is often perceived by students to be "an officially sanctioned school holiday" (Rossow & Parkinson, 1999, p. 39) and may be perceived to be a reward rather than a punishment by the offending student. This would appear to be especially true for students who have nothing to lose by being suspended because they were already failing in school.

If the desired outcome of out-of-school suspension is to reduce or eliminate student misbehavior and increase school safety, there is no empirical support for its effectiveness (Bacon, 1990; Bloomberg, 2004; Fenning & Bohanon, 2006; Skiba & Peterson, 2000). Instead of reducing or eliminating student misbehavior, some researchers have reported that students who are repeatedly suspended from school often return to school with the same or worse behaviors, whereas others have concluded that suspension appears to predict higher future rates of misbehavior and suspension among those students who are suspended and further alienates students (Ingersoll & Le Boeuf, 1997; Skiba et al., 2006; Slee, 1999). The ineffectiveness of suspensions in reducing or eliminating student misbehavior should not be surprising because the vast majority of students suspended from school, even repeatedly, do not receive any assistance in addressing those academic, social, or emotional issues that led to the incident for which the student was suspended (Raffaele Mendez, 2003).

Suspensions Are Correlated With a Number of Health and Social Problems

Suspensions have also been shown to be associated with a number of health and social problems. For example, youth who are not in school are more likely to have lower rates of academic achievement, to smoke, to use substances (e.g., alcohol, marijuana, cocaine), to engage in sexual intercourse, to

---

Box 1.1 Do Suspensions Work?

Suspensions have been shown to do the following:

- Predict higher rates of future misbehavior
- Alienate students
- Correlate with lower academic achievement
- Cause students to drop out
- Be ineffective in reducing misbehavior

---

become involved in physical fights, to carry a weapon, and are far more likely to commit crimes and be incarcerated (American Academy of Pediatrics, 2003; Wald & Losen, 2003). Many suspended students lack parental supervision, and suspended students repeat the same disruptive behaviors in the home and community (Ingersoll & Le Boeuf, 1997).

Suspensions have been shown to be a moderate to strong predictor of dropping out of school (Riordan, 2006; Skiba & Peterson, 2000), and dropping out in turn triples the likelihood that a person will be incarcerated later in life (Coalition for Juvenile Justice, 2001). One study found that students who have been suspended are three times more likely to drop out by the 10th grade than students who have never been suspended (Eckstrom, Goertz, Pollack, & Rock, 1986). Another study found that the number of out-of-school suspensions a student received as a sixth grader was correlated with the probability that the student would not graduate from high school with his or her cohort (Raffaele Mendez, 2003). One study reported that younger students were consistently more likely than older students to drop out of school for disciplinary reasons, with 11% of ninth graders leaving for disciplinary reasons (Stearns & Glennie, 2006). Box 1.1 lists a number of negative outcomes that have been shown to be associated with out-of-school suspensions.

Why Are So Many Students Being Suspended From School?

Given the growing numbers of suspensions and the detrimental outcomes associated with being suspended from school, it is increasingly important to understand the reasons why students are being suspended from school. There is some evidence that principals with more favorable attitudes toward suspension had higher rates of suspensions in their schools, compared to

---

principals who emphasized prevention and alternatives to suspension (Rausch & Skiba, 2004). Are out-of-school suspensions used for only serious and dangerous student offenses? A number of studies have concluded that suspensions are clearly not limited to only serious and dangerous offenses (Skiba & Rausch, 2006).

To answer this question using the most recent national data available, I examined the annual report entitled *Indicators of School Crime and Safety*, which is jointly issued by the National Center for Education Statistics and the Bureau of Justice Statistics. The report contains the most recent data available on school crime and student safety, including the reasons why students are seriously disciplined in schools. Data are based on information drawn from a variety of data sources, including national surveys of students, teachers, and principals (Dinkes, Kemp, & Baum, 2009). According to this national report, during the 2005–2006 school year, 48% of public schools (approximately 39,600 schools) reported taking at least one serious disciplinary action against students. Seventy-four percent of these disciplinary actions consisted of suspensions lasting 5 days or more, but less than the remainder of the school year, about 5 percent consisted of expulsions. The remaining 20% were transfers to specialized schools for disciplinary reasons. Figure 1.1 contains data on six specific student offenses that resulted in serious disciplinary actions for the 2005–2006 school year. As seen in Figure 1.1, the highest percentage of disciplinary actions taken by 83,200 public schools across the United States in 2005–2006 were in response to "physical attacks

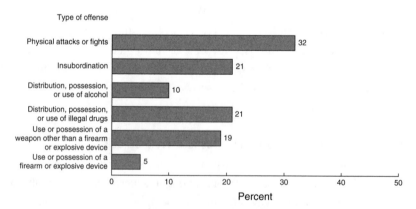

FIGURE 1.1 Percentage of public schools that took a serious disciplinary action for specific offenses, by type of offense: school year 2005–2006.

A New Model of School Discipline

or fights" (32%), and the second highest percentage (21%) was a tie between "distribution, possession, or use of illegal drugs" and "insubordination." Another relatively high percentage of public schools (19%) took a serious disciplinary action for "use or possession of a weapon other than a firearm or explosive device," whereas a relatively smaller percentage of public schools took a serious disciplinary action for "distribution, possession, or use of alcohol" (10%) and "use or possession of a firearm or explosive device" (5%).

It can also be seen in Figure 1.1 that six categories of offenses resulted in serious disciplinary actions in 2005–2006. Four of these categories of offenses (i.e., "physical attacks or fights"; "distribution, possession, or use of illegal drugs"; "distribution, possession, or use of alcohol"; and "use or possession of a firearm or explosive device"), which accounted for 68% of serious disciplinary actions by schools in 2005–2006, are clearly serious in nature or illegal. A short-term removal of the offending student for any of these four offenses would be considered a reasonable response.

However, a number of questions and concerns surround the remaining two categories of offenses contained in Figure 1.1 (i.e., "insubordination" and "use or possession of a weapon other than a firearm or explosive device"). It is important to raise these concerns and questions because these two categories of offenses accounted for a relatively high percentage (40%) of school removals in 2005–2006.

Concerns About "Insubordination"

The most serious concerns and questions are in relation to the category entitled "insubordination." In the report *Indicators of School Crime and Safety,* "insubordination" is defined as:

> A deliberate and inexcusable defiance of or refusal to obey a school rule, authority, or a reasonable order. It includes but is not limited to direct defiance of school authority, failure to attend assigned detention or on-campus supervision, failure to respond to a call slip, and physical or verbal intimidation/abuse. (Dinkes, Kemp, & Baum, 2009, p. 149)

The range of possible behaviors grouped under "insubordination" is very broad; therefore, it is difficult to determine the severity of a student's behavior that has resulted in suspension for this particular offense. While some behaviors included under this broad-ranging definition are clearly serious and warrant a serious disciplinary response, other behaviors are clearly less serious in nature. Should "failure to respond to a call slip" result in the same (or even similar) disciplinary action as "physical intimidation/abuse"? Are these two offenses even roughly equivalent in terms of severity? If not, why are they "lumped together" within the same category? The problem with "insubordination" is that it is a catchall category that includes both major and minor offenses yet deals with all offenses in the same harsh manner. It is not possible to distinguish between serious and relatively minor offenses within catchall categories. As long as school officials are provided with the option of reporting student behaviors under broadly defined catchall categories such as "insubordination," there will always be a question about whether a given student's behavior was serious enough to warrant a serious disciplinary response. It is also possible that a teacher or school administrator is misusing his or her authority to arbitrarily punish certain students, especially those students who continually challenge his or her authority. This is a serious concern that may account for large and growing numbers of suspensions, especially among poor and minority students. (This issue will be discussed in more detail later in this chapter.)

Another problem with characterizing certain student interactions with adults as "insubordination" is that this characterization fails to take into account the tolerance level of the adult as well as the context of a given adult–student interaction. For example, a student may openly challenge a statement made by one of his or her teachers and be praised by that teacher for his or her critical thinking, but that same student may challenge another teacher in a similar way and be written up by the second teacher for "insubordination."

Concerns About "Use or Possession of a Weapon Other Than a Firearm or Explosive Device"

At first glance, it would appear that the offense "use or possession of a weapon other than a firearm or explosive device" should always result in an automatic removal from school. For example, in the report *Indicators of School Crime and Safety,* weapons are defined as "guns, knives, and clubs" (Dinkes, Kemp, & Baum, 2009, p. 147), and there would be general agreement that if a student brought a gun, knife, or club to school, he or she should be removed from school. However, there is evidence that the definition of "weapons" may be much less certain than these concrete examples and open to interpretation in certain states and school districts. While no comprehensive review of how weapons are defined across states and school districts is currently available, a cursory examination of several states raises some questions and potential concerns. For example, Sughrue (2003) found that "weapons" in one Virginia school district was broadly defined to include "any instrument that could injure, harm or endanger the physical well being of another person." This definition goes on to list a wide number of objects that would be considered "weapons" but also includes the statement that weapons are "not limited to . . ." these objects (pp. 246–247). This author found that the definition of "weapon" in Tennessee public schools includes "razors and razor blades, except those used solely for personal shaving, and any sharp pointed or edged instrument, except unaltered nail files and clips and tools used solely for preparation of food, instruction and maintenance" (Tennessee Code).

A closer examination of several key words and phrases from these two state definitions raises some questions and concerns. For example, does *any instrument, any sharp pointed or edged instrument* mean that a sharpened pencil or pen could be considered a "weapon" in a given circumstance? How many and what types of objects could be considered to be "weapons" under the phrase *but is not limited to . . .* What objects would clearly not be considered to be "weapons"? Without this specificity about which specific objects are and which specific objects are not included in the definition of "weapon," there will always be a question about whether a given student's behavior in school was serious enough to warrant a serious disciplinary response such as suspension or expulsion. While findings from these two states cannot be generalized to other school districts across the United States, these preliminary findings illustrate the importance of further investigating the definition of "weapons" within individual states and school districts across the United States.

Concerns About Length of Suspensions and Repeated Suspensions

Another concern is the imprecise manner by which data on length of out-of-school suspensions is currently collected and reported in the *Indicators of School Crime and Safety* annual reports. Specifically, suspensions are reported as "consisting of suspensions *lasting 5 days or more, but less than the remainder of the school year.*" In other words, based on these data, we cannot tell if a student was suspended for as few as 5 days or for as many as 179 days (one day short of an entire school year) for a given offense. The severity of a 10-day suspension is very different from the severity of a suspension of 50 days. In essence, it is impossible to distinguish between short-term and long-term suspensions. This is a critical distinction because a long-term suspension is equivalent to an expulsion in terms of its educational impact on a student.

A related issue is the inability to determine how many times the same student is suspended during a school year. One study reported that as many as "40% of school suspensions are due to repeat offenders" (Skiba, 2000, p. 16), and multiple suspensions of a student have been strongly linked to an increased probability of dropping out (DeRidder, 1990; U.S. Department of Education, National Center for Education Statistics, 2006).

Concerns About Disproportionate Rates of Suspension of African American and Hispanic Students

A final and perhaps most troubling issue in examining the suspension data contained in the *Digest of Educational Statistics* for 2006 and 2008 (Snyder et al., 2007; Snyder et al., 2009) are the disproportionate rates of suspension of African American and Hispanic students compared to White students. While the percentage of White students suspended from school as a percentage of total enrollment was 4.9% in 2002 and decreased slightly to 4.8% in 2006, the percentage of African American students suspended from school as a percentage of total enrollment increased from an already high 13.9% in 2002 to 15% in 2006 (Snyder et al., 2007; Snyder et al., 2009). The percentage of Hispanic students suspended from school as a percentage of total enrollment increased from 6% in 2002 to 6.8% in 2006 (Snyder et al., 2007; Snyder et al., 2009). In other words, African American students were suspended at 2.8 times the rate of White students in 2002 and 3.1 times the rate of White students in 2006. Hispanic students were suspended at 1.2 times the rate of White students in 2002 and 1.4 times the rate of White students in 2006. These findings are consistent with other studies that have concluded that African American and Hispanic/Latino students are suspended from schools in disproportionate rates compared to White students (Brooks, Schiraldi & Ziedenberg, 2000; Bruns, Moore, Stephan, Pruitt, & Weist, 2005; Civil Rights Project at Harvard University, 2000; Raffaele Mendez & Knoff, 2003; Skiba, 2000; Skiba & Peterson, 2000). A recent study found that Black, Hispanic, and American Indian youth are two to five times more likely to be suspended or expelled compared to White and Asian American youth (Wallace, Goodkind, Wallace, & Bachman, 2008). This risk for suspension is particularly high for African American males from low socioeconomic status homes, particularly those in special education (Bruns, Moore, Stephan, Pruitt, & Weist, 2005; Raffaele Mendez & Knoff, 2003; Silka, Michael, & Nardo, 2000; Skiba, 2000).

Why are African American and Hispanic students at such increased risk of being suspended? Are these dramatic differences in suspension rates due to the fact that African American and Hispanic students commit much more serious offenses compared to White students? Are these differences due to the disparate ways that schools discipline African American and Hispanic students compared to White students? Unfortunately, the suspension data contained in Figure 1.1 is not broken down by race/ethnicity so it is not possible to address these questions based on these particular data. However, a number of other researchers have reported that African American and Hispanic/Latino students are suspended much more frequently for discretionary offenses, such as "defiance of authority" and "disrespect of authority" ("Opportunities suspended," 2000) and that the punishment that African American students receive is more frequent and harsher for similar or less serious offenses than White students (Raffaele-Mendez & Knoff, 2003; Skiba, 2000).

It can be argued that this disproportionality originates with referrals at the classroom level because students of color are more likely to be sent out of class with a disciplinary referral (Skiba, Michael, & Nardo, 2000). This often results when a teacher overreacts to a student who becomes defiant and gets into a power struggle with the student instead of de-escalating the situation. While a small minority of teachers are responsible for the vast majority of office referrals (Skiba, Peterson, & Williams, 1997), it must be recognized that many, if not most, teacher training programs do not provide teachers with the skills needed to manage the behavior of students from diverse backgrounds (Rausch & Skiba, 2004; Sullivan & Keeney, 2008). As a result, teachers are unfairly being expected to perform tasks for which they have not been adequately prepared. Unless this problem is addressed, suspensions of African American and Hispanic students are likely to increase in the future because our classrooms will continue to become more diverse. Specifically, in 2050, the population of children in the United States is projected to be 62% minority, up from 44% in 2008, and Hispanic children will comprise 39% of this increase (Bernstein & Edwards, 2008). Students with disabilities are also suspended and expelled at disproportionate rates. While students with disabilities typically represent between 11% and 14% of the student population in school districts, they comprise between 20% to

24% of the population of students who are suspended and expelled (Rausch & Skiba, 2006).

Corporal Punishment

While it receives little attention as a disciplinary practice today, corporal punishment remains legal in 21 states and it is used frequently in 13 states (see Box 1.2) (Human Rights Watch, 2008).

The Office for Civil Rights at the U.S. Department of Education reported that 223,190 students received corporal punishment at least once during the 2006–2007 school year in U.S. public schools (Human Rights Watch, 2008). Corporal punishment usually takes the form of paddling (also called "swats," "pops," or "licks"). Specifically, a teacher or administrator "swings a hard wooden paddle that is typically a foot-and-a-half long against the child's buttocks, anywhere between three and 10 times" (Human Rights Watch, 2008, p. 3). Corporal punishment is meted out more frequently among males, in rural areas of the United States, and among low-income children (Society for Adolescent Medicine, 2003). It also continues to be the sole choice of punishment in many elementary schools (Bauer, Dubanoski, Yamanachi, & Honbo, 1990) with the same students paddled over and over again (Teicher, 2005). African American students receive corporal punishment at a rate more

---

Box 1.2 States That Frequently Use Corporal Punishment

Alabama
Arkansas
Florida
Georgia
Kentucky
Louisiana
Mississippi
Missouri
North Carolina
Oklahoma
South Carolina
Tennessee
Texas

A New Model of School Discipline

than twice their proportion to the population (Global Progress, 2008). Approximately 15,000 students request medical treatment each year following instances of corporal punishment (Society for Adolescent Medicine, 2003).

There are no data demonstrating that the use of corporal punishment is associated with enhanced social skills or self-control skills over time (Society for Adolescent Medicine, 2003). Rather than resulting in more productive behaviors, studies have shown that students who are physically punished are more likely to engage in aggressive and violent behavior toward their siblings, parents, teachers, and peers in school (Human Rights Watch, 2008; Hyman & Perone, 1998). Corporal punishment has also been associated with increases in student absenteeism (Bauer et al., 1990), and the excessive use of corporal punishment has also been shown to be associated with conduct disorder in children and is comorbid with posttraumatic stress disorder (Hyman, 1995). Specific recommendations on how to address each of the issues raised in this chapter can be found in Chapter 4.

Summary

In summary, U.S. public schools have increasingly used out-of-school suspension in response to student misbehavior over the past decade. While most would agree that students should be excluded from school for dangerous offenses, there is overwhelming evidence that a growing number of students are suspended from school for relatively minor or subjectively defined (i.e., "insubordination") infractions. This is a particularly disturbing trend for African American and Hispanic students who are suspended at approximately three times the rate of White students. Students with disabilities are also suspended and expelled at disproportionate rates. There is no evidence that suspensions are effective in reducing or eliminating student misbehavior, and students who are repeatedly suspended from school often return to school with the same or worse behaviors following a suspension. Perhaps most troubling is the fact that suspensions have been shown to be a moderate to strong predictor of dropping out of school, and dropping out in turn triples the likelihood that a person will be incarcerated later in life. It is also important to note that current reporting methods for reporting school disciplinary infractions make it difficult to fully understand the cumulative impact of out-of-school suspensions on individual students because it is currently not possible to identify those students who are suspended repeatedly or to determine the length of each suspension. It is currently not possible to distinguish between short-term and long-term suspensions, and this is a critical distinction because a long-term suspension is equivalent to an expulsion in terms of its educational impact on a student.

Another school disciplinary practice that deserves much more scrutiny than it currently receives is corporal punishment. Corporal punishment remains legal in 21 states and is used frequently in 13 states. Studies have shown that corporal punishment is not only ineffective in long-term behavioral change but emotionally and physically harmful to students. As with suspensions, corporal punishment is used with African American students twice as often as White students.

2

■ ■ ■

How Did We Get Here? A Brief History of Discipline in U.S. Public Schools

According to the *American Heritage Dictionary of the English Language* (2000), definitions for the word *discipline* can be divided into two distinct categories. The first category of definitions reflects the original Latin root of the word *discipline*, which is "to learn" (Morrison & Skiba, 2001) by focusing on the development of self-control through the teaching of problem-solving skills and learning more productive ways to express feelings (i.e., "training expected to produce a specific character or pattern of behavior, especially training that produces moral or mental improvement," "self-control," and "to train by instruction and practice, especially to teach self-control.") The second category of definitions focuses on a reliance on external controls, submission to authority and punishment (i.e., "a state of order based on submission to rules and authority," "punishment intended to correct or train," "to teach to obey rules or accept authority," "to punish in order to gain control or enforce obedience," and "to impose order on"). How have these disparate definitions of *discipline* impacted discipline policies and practices in U.S. public schools over time?

In this chapter, I present a brief historical overview of several important forces that have shaped and continue to shape discipline in U.S. public schools. It includes a discussion of the profound impact of Puritanism over several centuries, major Supreme Court cases and federal and state legislation since the 1960s, and the impact of Department of Education (DOE) mandates and No Child Left Behind (NCLB) legislation. My discussion includes findings from a Government Accountability Office (GAO) report documenting alleged abuse, even death, resulting from the use of seclusion and restraints on students with disabilities in U.S. public schools as well as a case heard by the Supreme Court involving strip searches in public schools. I will then discuss a uniquely Western cultural phenomenon—the infantilization of our youth—and its impact on how adults think about youth and, in turn, how adults discipline them. I conclude this chapter by arguing that the current discipline paradigm in U.S. public schools is ineffective and harmful. A new way of thinking about school discipline is needed, as well as policies and practices that result from this new way of thinking. I will then discuss this in detail in Chapter 3.

From Puritanism to Zero Tolerance

Prior to the twentieth century, discipline was based on memorization of biblical teachings, fear of punishment, humiliation, and a sense of shame (Bear, Cavalier & Manning, 2002). Infants were viewed as inherently evil, and it was the parents' role to change the pleasure-loving child through quick, strong punishment (e.g., whipping) rather than "gentler" methods (e.g., scolding) (Wishy, 1968). Children were taught that by disobeying their parents they were forcing God to condemn them to eternal death and that obeying their parents would result in a better chance of salvation (Cable, 1975). The administration of corporal punishment has and continues to be strongly tied to and based upon a literal interpretation of the Bible, specifically Proverbs 23:13–14, which states "Do not withhold discipline from a child; if you punish him with the rod, he will not die. Punish him with the rod and save his soul from death." This discipline philosophy was also reflected in U.S. public schools, where teachers and school administrators, under the English common law concept of *in loco parentis* ("in place of the parent"), had the right not only to teach but to "maintain an orderly and effective learning environment through reasonable and prudent control of students" (Yell & Rozalski, 2008, p. 8).

This harsh and punitive discipline in schools continued until the early to mid-twentieth century when an emphasis on "threats, punishment, and religious education" was replaced by an emphasis on correcting and preventing school discipline problems through "character education" programs and their moral pronouncements about "right" and "wrong" (Bear, Cavalier, & Manning, 2002, p. 978). The 1990s brought yet another significant shift in school discipline policies and practices. In response to disastrous, yet relatively rare, instances of deadly school violence, Congress passed the *Gun-Free*

Schools Act (GFSA) in 1994. The GFSA mandated that each state must pass legislation that requires a 1-year expulsion for any student who brings a firearm to school in order to be eligible to receive certain federal education funding. This legislation resulted in the implementation of zero-tolerance policies and practices that have become the prevailing school discipline philosophy and paradigm in the vast majority of U.S. public schools over the past decade (Fenning & Bohanon, 2006; Skiba & Rausch, 2006). Many state legislatures and local school districts broadened the mandate of zero tolerance beyond the GFSA mandate on firearms to include offenses such as smoking, drugs and alcohol, fighting, threats, swearing, and the catchall category of "school disruption" (Skiba & Rausch, 2006). By the 1996–1997 school year, 94% of U.S. public schools had zero-tolerance policies for firearms, 91% for other weapons, 88% for drugs, and 87% for alcohol (Kaufman, et al., 2000).

A number of tenets and assumptions supporting a zero-tolerance philosophy of discipline (see Box 2.1) may not hold true for all students. For example, being excluded from school is not always viewed as a punishment by both the student and parent(s). Many at-risk students have "nothing to lose" by being excluded from school and would prefer not to be in school in order to avoid the constant failure they experience while in school. The parents of these students may not view their child's exclusion from school as a punishment either. For example, being excluded from school may be perceived as a "reward" or "vacation." Another assumption of a zero-tolerance discipline philosophy is that students know how to behave appropriately in school but choose not to.

Unfortunately, this is not the case for many at-risk students, who may lack the social skills and lack exposure to appropriate role models. For at-risk students, many of which are poor and minority, problematic behavior results from a discrepancy between the adaptive skills students need to survive in the school environment and those adaptive skills they currently possess (Schinke & Gilchrist, 1984). Repeatedly suspending students who do not have the necessary skills to behave appropriately in school will not result in more desirable behaviors. This is evidenced by the fact that students who are repeatedly suspended from school often return to school with the same or worse behaviors following a suspension (Slee, 1999). Assumptions about the nature of children and youth reflects a Puritanical belief that children and youth are "inherently evil" and in need of punishment and control by adults. It is assumed that students and parents should passively comply with the swift

Box 2.1 Zero-Tolerance Philosophy of School Discipline

Rationale	Students know how to act appropriately in school; punishing them by excluding them from school will send a strong message to the student and the student's parents that this misbehavior will not be tolerated; the student needs to return to school with more appropriate behaviors. Exclusion from school is viewed as a punishment by both the student and the parent because the student is being denied something he or she wants and has "something to lose" by being excluded from school.
Assumptions about students	All students have the tendency to misbehave if not restrained by adults.
School authorities' role	School discipline is based on fear of authority figures and external teacher controls; being mean is a necessary part of establishing authority and control. Students must earn the respect of teachers.
Student's role	Passive compliance to external controls
Parent's role	Accept and support school authority and discipline policies
Timing and consequences	Respond to all misbehavior with immediate and severe punishment, often involving exclusion (i.e., out-of-school suspension and expulsion)

Sources: Johnson, Whitington, & Oswald, 1994; Skiba et al. (n.d.); Watson & Battistich, 2006.

and severe punishment meted out by the school. Rather than viewing respect as a two-way street, zero-tolerance discipline relies heavily on fear and puts all the pressure on students to earn the respect of their teachers.

The pervasive impact of zero-tolerance discipline policies and practices in today's U.S. public schools cannot be overstated. The tough and swift "one-size-fits-all" punishment to student misbehavior often results in the removal of students from school through out-of-school suspension and expulsion (see Chapter 1). It has also forced schools to relinquish their role *in loco parentis* and expand their role as policemen (Sughrue, 2003, p. 256).

Legislation and Litigation Impacting Discipline in U.S. Public Schools

In addition, school discipline policies and practices have been impacted by a number of Supreme Court rulings over the past 40 years. In all of these rulings, the Court was faced with striking a balance between (a) school's right to maintain a safe and orderly environment through the reasonable and prudent control of students and (b) students' constitutional right to a public education, right to due process, right to privacy, and freedom from unreasonable searches (Education Law Center, 2007; Yell & Rozalski, 2008). The landmark decision of *Tinker v. Des Moines Independent Community School* (1969) focused on students' rights to freedom of expression while in school. In *Tinker*, the Supreme Court ruled that a student's right to freedom of expression "does not stop at the school house gate" and that "a student's nondisruptive personal expression that occurs in school is protected by the First Amendment even if the ideas are unpopular and controversial." In *Tinker,* the Court also ruled that "school officials do not possess absolute authority over their students" (p. 511). While several subsequent Supreme Court decisions have somewhat narrowed *Tinker*'s holding (see Schimmel, 2006), the central tenets of *Tinker* "remain good law" (Schimmel, 2006, p. 1006).

Another landmark Supreme Court decision was handed down in *Goss v. Lopez* (1975). *Goss v. Lopez* recognized that students have Constitutional and due process protections when they are subjected to certain disciplinary procedures, such as suspension. It also acknowledged that schools' disciplinary actions that result in a student being deprived of an education, for even 10 days, is a serious event in the life of the suspended child (Yell & Rozalski, 2008). In *Goss v. Lopez,* the Court stated that students have rights on disciplinary matters based on the due process clauses of the Fifth and Fourteenth Amendments to the U.S. Constitution. While acknowledging that schools have broad authority to prescribe and enforce standards of behavior, *Goss* ruled that students cannot be suspended without due process (i.e., a student must be told what he or she is accused of doing, the evidence against the student must be explained, and the student must be given a chance to explain his or her side of the story) (Yell & Rozalski, 2008). According to the high court, however, the "due process protections afforded to students are limited by states' interest in maintaining order and discipline in schools" (Yell & Rozalski, 2008, p. 10).

Several other Supreme Court cases have provided schools with "tools" they may use to maintain a safe and orderly environment. In *Ingraham v. Wright* (1977), the Supreme Court ruled that routine corporal punishment is not considered cruel and unusual punishment and does not violate procedural due process per se. (It should also be noted that since this ruling a majority of the states have enacted legislation outlawing the use of corporal punishment in public schools.) *New Jersey v. T.L.O.* (1985) was a seminal Court decision regarding searches of student property (Yell & Rozalski, 2008). In essence, this ruling acknowledges that while students have Constitutional protections against unreasonable searches, schools have a great deal of latitude to conduct searches as long as these searches are based on reasonable suspicion and are "not excessively intrusive' in light of the age and sex of the student and nature of the infraction" (Schimmel, 2006, p. 1008). Another Supreme Court ruling related to strip searches was decided in the summer of 2009. In *Safford Unified School District #1 v. Redding*, the Supreme Court ruled that Arizona school officials violated the constitutional rights of a 13-year old girl when they strip-searched her based on the suspicion that she was hiding ibuprofen in her underwear (Barnes, 2009).

Despite the fact individual state laws, rather than federal laws, largely control the actions of school officials in carrying out discipline in U.S. public schools, some important federal legislation has and continues to impact school discipline in important ways. In addition to the GFSA of 1994 (discussed previously in this chapter), several provisions of the NCLB Act of 2001 and mandates from the U.S. DOE provide further guidance, sometimes through contradictory messages, regarding the development of school discipline policies and practices (Sullivan & Keeney, 2008). On the one hand, the DOE mandates that schools should get tough by punishing and removing students, but the NCLB uses high suspension rates as one criteria for labeling schools as "persistently dangerous" and penalizes schools that receive this label. It can also be argued that the NCLB has had an indirect impact on school discipline by pressuring teachers to raise test scores as well as maintain order. With these pressures "come more directive and punitive control strategies" (Woolfolk Hoy & Weinstein, 2006, p. 209). The NCLB also protects teachers who take reasonable actions to maintain order and discipline against litigation as a result of their actions (Woolfolk Hoy & Weinstein, 2006).

Individuals with Disabilities Education Act (IDEA) also impacts the ways in which schools may discipline students with disabilities. The procedural requirements of the IDEA (2004) grant students with disabilities more extensive due process rights than students without disabilities (Yell & Rozalski, 2008). However, these federal protections are largely limited to the suspension or expulsion of students with disabilities. (See Yell & Rozalski, 2008, for a detailed discussion of the legal rights of students with disabilities in relation to short-term and long-term suspensions.) However, beyond suspension and expulsion, students with disabilities can be disciplined in the same manner as students without disabilities (Yell & Rozalski, 2008). This is an important issue because a report by the GAO (2009) found that there are no federal laws restricting the use of seclusion and restraints in public and private schools and that there are widely divergent laws at the state level. This disturbing report found that "children, especially those with disabilities, are reportedly being restrained and secluded in public and private schools and other facilities, sometimes resulting in injury and death" (GAO, 2009, p. 7). The report documented hundreds of cases of alleged abuse and death that have occurred during the past two decades, including cases where "students were pinned to the floor for hours at a time, handcuffed, locked in closets, and subjected to other acts of violence" (GAO, 2009). Federal and state legislation and litigation has resulted in two overriding fundamental prerequisites that teachers and school officials must adhere to in developing rules and imposing disciplinary procedures in U.S. public schools. First, all students and their parents must understand what is not permitted, and disciplinary consequences for rule violations must be clearly stated and understood by all students and their parents. Second, disciplinary consequences must be applied on a fair and consistent basis and, in cases of suspension, students must be given notice of the offense that they have committed and be given an opportunity to tell their side of the story (Yell & Rozalski, 2008).

Our Infantilized "Adolescents"

An underexamined but significant cultural development over the past hundred years or so provides a compelling explanation for the oppositional and openly defiant behavior of young people. It is argued that youth misbehavior is correlated to the extent which a society delays or bans youth from adult activities and opportunities to develop adult attitudes and adult behavior; in other words, the extent to which youth are "infantilized" (Skager, 2007).

Throughout most of recorded human history, what we refer to today as the "teenage years" were a relatively peaceful time of transition to adulthood with little reported aggressive youth behavior. In preindustrial societies, young people, rather than spending the majority of their time with peers, spent the majority of their time with same-sex adults learning to become adults and "merging seamlessly into mature adult roles" (Epstein, 2007; Moshman, 1999; Schlegel & Barry, 1991; Skager, 2007). It has been suggested that much of the turmoil among teens in the United States today results from the ways in which we have reduced the status of our youth over the past hundred years. In fact, the word *teenager* did not even appear in print until 1941 (Skager, 2007). By inventing *adolescence* and viewing it as a period of life that is distinctly different from adulthood, we have artificially extended childhood past the onset of puberty and, as a result, harmed adult–youth relationships (Epstein, 2007; Skager, 2007). This is because defining *adolescence* as a distinct state of development results in treating young people much differently than adults (Skager, 2007). According to Epstein (2007), "teens in the U.S. are subjected to more than 10 times as many restrictions as are mainstream adults, twice as many as active-duty U.S. Marines, and even twice as many restrictions as incarcerated felons" (p. 59). In essence, adults have failed to draw a line between offensive student behavior and student behavior that results from the "natural need of teenagers to define themselves by testing limits" (Berger, 2008, p. 1). It is no wonder that we see much oppositional and defiant behavior among today's youth in our schools and communities. The ways in which we punish our youth in schools also serve to perpetuate the view that our youth are inferior beings who need to be tamed and controlled (Kimmel, n.d.). Epstein eloquently describes the unique and troubling situations facing today's teens:

> Today, with teens trapped in the frivolous world of peer culture, they learn virtually everything they know from one another rather than from the people they are about to become. Isolated from adults and wrongly treated like children, it is no wonder that some teens behave, by adult standards, recklessly or irresponsibly. Almost without exception, the reckless and irresponsible behavior we see is the teen's way of declaring his or her adulthood or, through pregnancy or the commission of serious crime, of instantly *becoming* an adult under the law. Fortunately, we also know from extensive research both in the U.S. and elsewhere that when we treat teens like adults, they almost immediately rise to the challenge. (p. 63)

I agree with these authors that much oppositional and defiant behavior in teens today results from their constant exposure to other teens rather than adults. This constant exposure to peers serves to exacerbate and reinforce behaviors that adults forbid or discourage, including using drugs or getting drunk, having sex, dressing bizarrely, and getting tattoos and body piercings (Skager, 2007). In turn, these oppositional behaviors have resulted in increasingly punitive responses to youth misbehavior in schools, law enforcement, and even in the mental health system. Many school administrators have readily relinquished school discipline to "law enforcement officers who inhabit the hallways and other public areas of schools these days" (Sughrue, 2003, p. 256). We criminalize youth behavior by making more and more of their activities explicitly illegal (Skager, 2007). Within the mental health system, the *Diagnostic and Statistical Manual of Mental Disorders* defines oppositional defiant disorder (ODD) with criteria (i.e., "often argues with adults," "deliberately annoys people," and "is often touchy") that can be used "to justify treatment (and prescription of psychoactive drugs to get the young person under control) for behaviors not uncommon among infantilized teenagers" (Skager, 2007, p. 3).

There is a need to fundamentally change the way that we discipline students in schools. In order to make this change we need to alter the way that we think about discipline and the adequacy of the current paradigm upon which our discipline policies and practices have been built. In Chapter 3, I present a case for making a paradigmatic shift in how we think about discipline and how we discipline students in schools.

Summary

Throughout most of its history, discipline in U.S. public schools has relied upon punishment and submission to authority. There is much evidence to support the argument that the current discipline paradigm is ineffective, harms students, and exacerbates the dropout problem. The implementation of zero-tolerance policies and practices over the past decade has resulted in a continuation of this punitive discipline philosophy in today's public schools. Unfortunately, a number of tenets and assumptions supporting a zero-tolerance philosophy of discipline do not hold true for students who are at risk of school failure. For too many students the current discipline paradigm in U.S. public schools is ineffective, harmful, and contributes to the decision to drop out of school.

A number of Supreme Court rulings over the past 40 years have shaped school discipline in important ways by addressing the balance between the school's right to maintain a safe and orderly environment and the student's Constitutional right to a public education, right to due process, right to privacy, and freedom from unreasonable searches. Federal legislation has also impacted school discipline in important ways.

The infantilization of our youth in today's society provides a compelling explanation for the oppositional and openly defiant behavior of young people. It has important implications for changing the ways in which we discipline children and youth in our schools.

3

■ ■ ■

A New Paradigm: A Relationship-Based, Preventive Model of Discipline

Thus far, I have discussed a number of problems with the current school discipline paradigm/philosophy. In Chapters 1 and 2, I argued that the current discipline paradigm in U.S. public schools is ineffective and responds to student misbehavior by punishing and criminalizing students. Indeed, there is a pressing need for a fundamental paradigmatic shift in the way that we think about school discipline and the ways in which schools develop discipline policies and practices. In this chapter, I describe a new school discipline paradigm that is comprehensive, preventive, and based on enhancing relationships. I argue that we need to think about school discipline as a complex and interactive process involving a number of school contextual factors, and I discuss those factors that impact student behavior. I emphasize the importance of school connectedness in reducing discipline problems, and I highlight five school characteristics that are important in assessing the extent to which students feel "connected" to their school. I conclude this chapter with a discussion of assumptions and central tenets of this new relationship-based, preventive model of school discipline.

School Discipline Is a Complex Process

Before designing an effective disciplinary system, it is important to understand the interactive nature and complexity that underlies student misbehavior. Student behavior is shaped by a series of internal and external factors. Internally, physical, developmental, and emotional factors often drive student behavior "without students fully understanding what the consequences might be" (Richart, Brooks, & Soler, 2003, p. 27). Externally, school and classroom climate and interactions with peers and adults can also produce problematic behavior (Noguera, 2001). The failure to acknowledge this complex interplay of factors may help to explain why current school disciplinary approaches are largely ineffective—school officials that single out students rather than addressing the school contextual factors that contribute to student misbehavior (Rathvon, 1999). Rather than limiting our view of discipline problems to internal child deficits, we need to acknowledge this complex interaction and view student behavior problems as the result of student–environment mismatches (Rathvon, 1999). This is especially true for African American and Hispanic students, who receive a disproportionate number of suspensions and expulsions. Which school factors appear to contribute to student–environment mismatches and may exacerbate student misbehavior?

School Factors That Impact Student Misbehavior

Not surprisingly, teacher attitudes and behavior are very important. For example, it has been reported that negative teacher attitudes toward students generally emerge within the first few weeks of classes and that these attitudes tend to remain stable (Safran & Safran, 1985). Classroom behavior problems can result when teachers unknowingly dominate classroom communication, rely on repetitive seat work, or lack insight into how their personal beliefs and behaviors toward students may inhibit students' academic performance or aggravate students' behavior (Erchul & Martens, 1997). Academic demands also contribute to student–environment mismatches. For example, students who are struggling academically are more likely to engage in rebellious or hostile behavior (Brantlinger, 1995).

Of all the factors discussed in the literature, the "connection" between students and schools appears to be essential. In general, it has been shown that higher levels of school attachment, school commitment, and belief in school rules were found to be associated with lower levels of misbehavior in school (McNeely, Nonnemaker, & Blum, 2002; Stewart, 2003). A number of concepts have been used in the literature to describe this important "connection," including *school engagement, school attachment, school bonding, school involvement,* and *school connectedness* (Libbey, 2004). For the purposes of this chapter, I will use the term *school connectedness*. Students who report feeling more connected to school show lower levels of emotional distress, risk behavior, and aggression (Ozer, 2005). There is evidence that as students grow older, they feel less attached to school. This decline in student engagement and motivation is especially noticeable as students move from elementary school to middle school (McNeely, Nonnemaker, & Blum, 2002), and it has been linked to student behavior problems (Centers for Disease Control and Prevention, 2009). *School connectedness* has been defined as "the belief by students that adults and peers in the school care about their learning as well as about them as individuals" (Centers for Disease Control and Prevention, 2009, p. 3).

Five school characteristics are important in assessing the extent to which students feel "connected" to their school. These school characteristics are school and classroom climate, severity of discipline policies, relationships with peers and teachers, school size, and rates of participation in extracurricular activities (McNeely, Nonnemaker, & Blum, 2002; National Longitudinal Study of Adolescent Health, 2006). Each of these characteristics will be discussed in turn. First and foremost, the climate of a school and classrooms within a school play an important role in connecting students with schools. A number of factors have been shown to contribute to building and maintaining a positive school climate (see Box 3.1).

A positive school climate includes a variety of characteristics, including the physical layout of the school, but the primary focus is on the meaningful involvement of students in all aspects of their education, clear rules and high expectations for behavior, and the strengthening of teacher–student relationships. Since large differences between classrooms often exist in the same school (Bear & Smith, 2009), it is also important to pay attention to factors that have been shown to contribute to building and maintaining a positive classroom climate (see Box 3.2).

Students are more connected and engaged in classrooms where teachers are empathic, respectful, consistent, and clear about what they expect from students. A classroom climate is more positive when teachers make the effort to connect with each student in some way and emphasize cooperation rather than competition. It is also important that teachers make students responsible for their own behavior and help student learn from mistakes (e.g., "mistakes are learning experiences").

Another characteristic that has been shown to be important in assessing the extent to which students feel "connected" to their school is students' perception of school discipline policies and practices. It has been reported that student connectedness is lower in schools with harsh and punitive discipline policies than schools with more moderate discipline policies (McNeely, Nonnemaker, & Blum, 2002).

Another characteristic associated with school connectedness is caring and supportive relationships among peers and between teachers and students

Box 3.1 Factors That Contribute to a Positive School Climate

- The school has an attractive and inviting physical landscape.
- Intentional efforts are made to build and maintain caring, respectful, supportive, and collaborative relationships among school staff members, students, and families.
- Both students and staff experience school as meaningful, productive, and relevant.
- Student participation in decision making is emphasized.
- Students perceive rules as being clear, fair, and not overly harsh.
- Students, families, and teachers perceive the school as safe.
- Service learning opportunities are available.
- Schools have high academic and behavioral expectations and provide the necessary supports to achieve these expectations.
- Intentional efforts are made to develop social and emotional competencies among all students.
- Educators model and nurture an attitude that emphasizes the benefits of, and satisfaction from, learning.
- Parents and community members are viewed as valuable resources, and their active involvement with schools is encouraged.

Sources: Aspy & Roebuck, 1977; Battistich & Hom, 1997; Bear & Smith, 2009; Centers for Disease Control and Prevention, 2009; Fredricks, Blumenfeld, & Paris, 2004; Freiberg & Lapointe, 2006; Freiberg, Stein, & Huang, 1995; Grossman & Bulle, 2006; McNeely, Nonnemaker, & Blum, 2002; Noguera, 2001; Ryan & Patrick, 2001; Wilson, 2004.

(Battistich & Hom, 1997; Wilson, 2004). Students who report feeling most connected to school also report having the most friends at school, rather than out of school, and having friends from several different social groups that are integrated by race and gender. Conversely, when friendship patterns are

Box 3.2 Factors That Contribute to a Positive Classroom Climate

- Teachers who are empathic and consistent
- Teachers who set routines and guidelines
- Teachers who administer fair consequences for misbehaviors
- Classrooms where expectations for individual responsibility are clear and consistent
- Teachers that encourage student self-management
- Teachers that provide daily opportunities for meaningful student participation and decision making
- Teachers who consistently acknowledge all students
- A classroom that emphasizes cooperation (rather than competition)
- Teachers who promote mutual respect in the classroom

Sources: Aspy & Roebuck, 1977; Battistich & Hom, 1997; Centers for Disease Control and Prevention, 2009; Fredricks, Blumenfeld, & Paris, 2004; Freiberg & Lapointe, 2006; Freiberg, Stein, & Huang, 1995; Grossman & Bulle, 2006; McNeely, Nonnemaker, & Blum, 2002; Noguera, 2001; Ryan & Patrick, 2001; Wilson, 2004.

segregated by race, students from all racial groups feel less connected to school (McNeely, Nonnemaker, & Blum, 2002).

In addition to positive peer relationships, there is growing recognition that positive teacher–student relationships increase students' connectedness with school and improve classroom discipline. A critical developmental need of all students is the development of a strong, positive relationship with a caring adult (Comer, 2001). This is especially important for children and youth of color and those from lower socioeconomic backgrounds (Metz, 1983). Teachers clearly play a pivotal role in the 'disciplinary chain' that occurs in public schools. They frequently 'make the decision—often in a split second—whether to keep an incident contained within the classroom or whether to instigate the disciplinary referral that could lead to suspension' (Wald & Casella, 2006, p. 90). This decision is often compounded by potential cultural conflicts and misunderstandings between middle-class teachers and students of color and poor students. For example, Caucasian teachers and principals sometimes misunderstand or mis-construe the more active and physical communication style common among poor and minority youth, particularly African American youth (Raffaele Mendez

& Knoff, 2003; Skiba, Michael, Nardo, & Peterson, 2002; Vavrus & Cole, 2002). The impassioned and emotive manner popular among young African Americans may be interpreted as combative or argumentative by unfamiliar listeners (Townsend, 2000) and may result in teachers overreacting to relatively minor threats to authority. As Gay (2006) noted, "many students of color, especially in middle and high schools, are not willing to passively submit to the demands of teachers for immediate and unquestioning compliance in conflict situations, especially if they feel they are treated unfairly and denied the opportunity to defend themselves" (p. 353). Instead of de-escalating the situation, teachers may engage in power struggles with students that often result in a disciplinary referral and a trip to school administrators who spend hundreds of hours responding to disciplinary referrals sent to the office (Gottfredson, Gottfredson, & Hybl, 1993).

The importance of "teachers' being warm, responsive, caring, and supportive as well as holding high expectations ('warm demanders') appears frequently in the literature" (Evertson & Weinstein, 2006, p. 11). According to Skager (2007), "the basic principle in achieving positive relationships between adults and young people is treating them with respect" (p. 3). One of the most powerful ways of showing respect is by listening to young people and participating in two-way conversations in which young people participate as equals (Skager, 2007). Teacher–student relationships are also enhanced through informal interactions with youth and having interests, culture, or backgrounds in common with youth (Grossman & Bulle, 2006). The potential impact of teacher–student connections is stated forcefully by Woolfolk Hoy & Weinstein (2006):

> Teachers need to recognize that to teach well, they must also put effort into forging positive relationships with students. The research clearly demonstrates the link between positive student–teacher relationships and students' motivation to become engaged with academic activities. As Valenzuela (1999) points out, for some students at least, being cared *for* is a precondition of *caring* about school. When students see schooling as irrelevant to their futures, when schools seem to denigrate their culture or language, or when noncompliance seems to be the best way to resist coercion, then the only thing that will bring these resistant and reluctant students into the fold of education might be the power of human connection and caring. (p. 210)

- School and classroom climate
- Severity of discipline policies
- Relationships with peers and teachers
- School size
- Rates of participation in extracurricular activities

School size has also been found to be associated with school connectedness. For example, "on average, students in smaller schools feel more attached to school than students in larger schools ... several researchers suggest that large school size negatively affects school connectedness because, in such settings, teachers cannot maintain warm, positive relations with all students." Class size, however, was not associated with school connectedness (McNeely, Nonnemaker, & Blum, 2002, p. 145).

A fifth and final characteristic found to be associated with school connectedness is rates of participation in extracurricular activities. Schools that have higher rates of participation in extracurricular activities during or after school tend to have higher levels of school connectedness (Blum, McNeely, & Rinehart, 2002; Centers for Disease Control and Prevention, 2009; Grossman & Bulle, 2006). These findings on school connectedness are essential in conceptualizing and implementing a new model of school discipline. See Box 3.3 for a list of characteristics that have been shown to be important in connecting students to their school.

A New Model of School Discipline: Relationship-Based, Preventive Discipline

The new model of school discipline that I discuss here is based on the assumption that enhancing relationships and teaching students the "skills they will need to get along in school and society" should form the basis of all school discipline (Skiba, Ritter, Simmons, Peterson, & Miller, 2006, p. 631). Specifically, it teaches students how to solve interpersonal and intrapersonal problems in productive ways (Skiba & Peterson, 2000). It is a discipline model that is built upon caring and trust, dignity and cooperation, and that communicates to all students that they are respected and valued members of the school community (Belenardo, 2001; Freiberg & Lapointe, 2006). It is a discipline model that views discipline as "teachable moments" that provide students with an opportunity for learning and growth (Sullivan & Keeney, 2008). It is a discipline model that is preventive in nature; it anticipates the inevitable conflicts that occur on a daily basis in schools and implements strategies designed to defuse rather than escalate these interpersonal conflicts. It is a discipline model that acknowledges that there is no one simple solution to problems of school disruption and, therefore, a comprehensive range of effective strategies as well as a partnership of school, family, and community are required (Skiba, Ritter, et al., 2006). It is a discipline model that utilizes social learning theory to teach social, behavioral, and cognitive skills to children and youths using structured skill-training techniques and lesson plans (Jenson, 2006). It is also a discipline model that reflects a human rights perspective that includes the right to be free from discrimination, the right to education, the right to proportionality in punishment, and the right to freedom of expression (Dignity in Schools Campaign, 2008). In essence, a relationship-based, preventive model of school discipline creates an environment in which students "behave appropriately, not out of fear of punishment or desire for reward, but out of a sense of personal responsibility, respect, and regard for the group" (Woolfolk Hoy & Weinstein, 2006, p. 210).

A relationship-based, preventive model of school discipline should be based upon a response to intervention (RtI) framework. RtI is a comprehensive, multitiered system of delivering evidence-based services to students that utilizes a problem-solving approach and offers increasing levels of support based on increasing levels of student needs (Samuels, 2009). Specifically, the first tier (universal) consists of interventions that are provided to all students, the second tier (targeted group) consists of interventions that specifically target behaviorally at-risk students, and the third tier (intensive individualized) consists of interventions developed for students who need more intensive, individualized attention/services. Box 3.4 lists the major tenets of a relationship-based, preventive model of school discipline.

A relationship-based, preventive model of school discipline focuses heavily on equipping students with the knowledge and skills necessary to handle conflict in an encouraging and supportive manner. There is also an emphasis on utilizing best practices in preventing discipline problems in schools. In the next chapter, I will identify and describe these best practices and what works in preventing school discipline problems in much greater detail.

Summary

There is a pressing need for a fundamental paradigmatic shift in the way that we think about school discipline and the ways in which schools develop discipline policies and practices. An effective model of school discipline acknowledges that discipline is a complex process that involves both internal and external factors. The failure to acknowledge this complex interplay of factors and student–environment mismatches may explain why current school disciplinary approaches are largely ineffective. A number of school factors may contribute to and even exacerbate student misbehavior, including teacher attitudes and behavior, academic demands, and student disengagement.

A new model of discipline should draw from findings on school connectedness because the "connection" between students and schools has been shown to be strongly associated with lower levels of student misbehavior. Five school characteristics are important in assessing the extent to which students feel "connected" to their school: school and classroom climate, severity of discipline policies, relationships with peers and teachers, school size, and rates of participation in extracurricular activities. This new model of school discipline focuses on enhancing relationships and teaching students the skills they will need to get along in school and society. It is a model built upon trust and dignity and one that views school discipline as "teachable moments." It is a discipline model that incorporates best practices in reducing or preventing school discipline problems, and utilizes a response to intervention (RtI) framework in developing and delivering services to students.

4

■ ■ ■

Best Practices in Reducing or Preventing Student Behavior Problems: Multitiered Programs and Strategies

A new proactive, preventive model of discipline based on enhancing relationships and connecting students with schools requires a comprehensive multitiered approach. Rather than a "one-size-fits-all," prescribed model, in this chapter, I identify and describe an array of empirically supported programs and strategies at each of the three intervention levels (i.e., primary/universal, secondary/targeted, and tertiary/remedial). These are designed to meet the unique needs of an individual school district in the most effective, pragmatic, and cost-efficient manner possible.

I begin this chapter by discussing widely used school security measures that have not been empirically supported in improving school climate or reducing student behavior problems. I then make a series of recommendations for improving the ways in which school discipline data are collected and reported to the general public. Most importantly, I present a rationale for developing and implementing comprehensive, multitiered interventions to reduce behavior problems in schools. To this end, I briefly catalog an array of empirically supported strategies and programs at each intervention level designed to meet the needs of students.

Why Evidence-Based Interventions?

In this age of increasing accountability and scrutiny, it is important for school officials to select interventions based upon the best available scientific evidence. This conscientious use of current best evidence is referred to as evidenced-based practice (EBP). The experimental rigor and criteria for determining the extent to which a program or strategy can be considered "evidence-based" has been proposed by different organizations including the What Works Clearinghouse. At a minimum, evidence-based practices or interventions are those that provide the following: (a) an explicit description of the procedure/practice; (b) a clear definition of the settings and implementers who use the procedure/practice; (c) the identification of the population of individuals who are expected to benefit; and (d) the specific outcomes expected ("Is School-wide Positive Behavior Support an Evidence-based Practice?" 2009). Among the most rigorous standards for documenting that a practice/procedure is evidence-based is demonstration of at least two peer-reviewed randomized control trial research studies that document experimental control ("Is School-wide Positive Behavior Support an Evidence-based Practice?" 2009) Evidenced-based practice is a process for handling uncertainty in an honest and informed manner, sharing ignorance as well as knowledge (Chalmers, 2003). A number of systematic steps have been identified in the implementation of EBP (Gibbs & Gambrill, 1999). Readers are encouraged to read Dupper (2007) and Raines (2008) for a detailed description of the EBP process.

In the following section, I identify and describe an array of programs and strategies with at least some empirical evidence that they are effective in improving school climate and/or reducing student behavior problems. However, these programs and strategies vary widely in terms of their empirical support. Some have undergone rigorous and extensive evaluations and can be considered "proven," while others can only be characterized as "promising." Readers are encouraged to keep up with new research findings by routinely searching databases and Web sites that contain research findings and best practice guidelines for improving school climates and reducing student behavior problems. Fortunately, a growing number of databases are available online and can be accessed from home computers or laptops connected to the Internet. Important databases that can be accessed online include ERIC, Social Sciences Citation Index, Dissertation Abstracts, PsycINFO, and Web of Science. These databases contain abstracts of refereed journal articles and books. The Campbell Collaboration (http://www.campbellcollaboration.org) and the Cochrane Collaboration (http://www.cochrane.org) contain systematic reviews of research studies, and the What Works Clearinghouse (http://www.ies.ed.gov/ncee/wwc) is a source of scientific evidence for what works in education.

Do Widely Used School Security Measures "Work?"

To begin our discussion, it is important to identify and discuss those interventions that are currently used by schools across the United States and to determine which of these interventions, if any, should be included as part of a new comprehensive model of school discipline designed to improve school climate and reduce behavior problems. This discussion focuses on the extent to which there is empirical evidence that a particular intervention is effective in achieving these desired outcomes.

School districts across the United States are increasingly using a number of security measures. Measures such as locked or monitored doors or gates are designed to limit or control access to school campuses, while measures such as metal detectors, security cameras, and drug sweeps are designed to monitor or restrict students' and visitors' behavior on campus. During the 2005–2006 school year, 85% of public schools limited access to school buildings by locking or monitoring doors during school hours; 41% limited access to school grounds with locked or monitored gates; 48% of public schools required faculty and staff to wear badges or picture identification; and 43% used one or more security cameras (Dinkes, Kemp, & Baum, 2009). While several studies have reported that metal detectors led to a reduction in weapons at school, no studies to date have demonstrated a causal relationship between these specific security procedures and a reduction in school violence (Mayer & Leone, 2007).

This also holds true for the popular school resource officer programs. While a number of studies have concluded that that SROs are viewed favorably by school personnel and parents and, to a lesser extent by students, "no study has demonstrated a causal link showing that SRO programs reduce school violence and disruption" (Mayer & Leone, 2007, p. 12).

In addition to these security measures, a growing but still relatively small number of schools are requiring students to wear school uniforms as a means of reducing student misbehavior. According to Peterson (2008), school uniform policies typically require all students to wear clothing that meets specific criteria, such as color of clothing, type of pants, and length of a skirt. In 2005–2006, 14% of public schools required students to wear uniforms. Most of the research on school uniform policies has assessed perceptions of teachers, administrators, parents, and students of the usefulness of these policies rather than using direct behavioral measures to assess the effectiveness of these policies. Despite supportive testimonials and anecdotal reports, there are no reported studies that demonstrate that school uniforms have any effect on reducing student behavior problems (Peterson, 2008).

Before any of these strategies be considered as part of a comprehensive discipline program, it is essential that scientifically rigorous studies be conducted to determine whether these widely implemented strategies are effective in improving school climate and reducing behavior problems.

State-Wide and District-Level Recommendations

In Chapter 1, I raised serious concerns about the current methods used to gather, categorize, and report school-level and state-wide school disciplinary data to the general public. Any comprehensive program designed to prevent or reduce student behavior problems and improve school climates should address these concerns. For example, it is often difficult to discern what the student actually did that resulted in a disciplinary action as well as to assess the extent to which a school's disciplinary response was justified in individual cases. For example, there is no way to know what students actually did when they were written up for a catchall category such as "insubordination". While one student may have actively attempted to undermine the teacher's authority in a classroom situation, another student may have failed to look a teacher in the eye while being spoken to. Yet both students could be written up under "insubordination." While a disciplinary response in the former situation may be justified, it would be much more difficult to justify a similar disciplinary response to the latter situation. The central problem with catchall categories of infractions such as insubordination is that no one knows what the student actually did and if the student's action warranted a certain disciplinary action (Theriot & Dupper, in press). To remedy this problem, catchall categories such as insubordination should not be used in reporting disciplinary offenses. Rather, states and local school districts should gather and report data that clearly define what students did as well as specific information on any disciplinary action taken by the school and the duration of the disciplinary action.

As a general rule, disciplinary consequences should be geared to the seriousness of the student's infraction with exclusionary practices such as suspensions and expulsions reserved for only the most serious and disruptive student behaviors. Since a long-term suspension is equivalent to an expulsion in terms of its educational impact on a student, the number of days that a student is suspended out of school should correspond to the seriousness of the student's offense. To ensure that this occurs, school discipline codes should be reviewed by panels that include students, parents, and all members of the school community. Relatively minor, low-level student offenses (e.g., sleeping in class, being out of one's seat without permission) should not be allowed to accumulate over time and should be dealt with by the classroom teacher rather than by administrative referral. District-wide teacher training in how to implement culturally sensitive classroom management strategies that focus on de-escalating inevitable daily conflicts should be mandated and a part of teachers' annual evaluations. Finally, all school discipline policies and procedures should be evaluated to ensure that they have reduced student misbehavior (Skiba & Rausch, 2006).

Why Multitiered Interventions?

Within any school setting, three groups of students can be identified: (a) about 75%–85% are typically developing students who show no signs of significant behavioral or emotional problems, (b) about 10%–15% are students at risk for developing behavioral and emotional problems, and (c) 3%–5% of students show signs of severe mental health problems, delinquent activities, violence, and/or vandalism (Larson, 1995; Moffitt, 1994; Walker et al., 1995). These three groups of students lie along a risk continuum, where differing types of intervention that vary by specificity, complexity, comprehensiveness, expense, and intensity may be provided (Reid, 1993). For example, students who do not respond to a primary/universal intervention may require more intensive interventions at the secondary/targeted level. Similarly, students who do not respond to a secondary/targeted intervention would require more powerful and intensive interventions at the tertiary/remedial level (Skiba, Ritter, et al., 2006). This multitiered system of delivering services allows for the early identification of students who are struggling with behavior problems, and it bases the delivery of services on student needs (Samuels, 2009).

Skiba, Boone, Fontanini, Strussell, & Peterson (n.d.) outline several important assumptions that should guide the development and implementation of a multitiered, prevention approach to school discipline:

1. Serious and violent student behavior is preventable, and schools must do everything they can on a daily basis to reduce the risk that minor incidents and disruptions will escalate into serious violence and result in suspensions or expulsions.

2. No single strategy is effective in reducing student misbehavior and violence.
3. Effective prevention programs require a proactive approach that involves ongoing planning, commitment, and collaboration among school staff, parents, and the community.

As discussed in Chapter 3, this multitiered delivery system is based on a response-to-intervention (RtI) framework designed to deliver "scientific, data-based methods into schools and classrooms to guide the selection, use, and evaluation of academic and behavioral interventions" (Greene, 2008, pp. 57–58). In this conceptualization, prevention and intervention are not viewed as distinct or mutually exclusive dimensions; rather, different types of interventions and approaches are used to achieve specific prevention goals and outcomes (Larson, 1994). These multitiered interventions largely define the social and emotional "curriculum" of schools (Morrison, Blood, & Thorsborne, 2005).

Proven and Promising Primary/Universal Programs and Strategies

Programs and strategies at the primary/universal level "target all members of the school community through an 'immunization' strategy; such that all members of the school community develop social and emotional skills to resolve conflict in caring and respectful ways" (Morrison et al,, 2005, p. 349). Primary/universal strategies target all students in the same manner. A number of primary/universal programs have been developed, widely implemented, and evaluated over the past several decades and found to be effective in effective in improving school climates and a relationship-based, preventive approach to school discipline. These programs include the following: the *Child Development Project* (Greenberg et. al., 2000); the *School Development Program* (Gottfredson, 2001); *Second Step* (Larson, 1994); *Resolving Conflicts Creatively Program* (DeJong, 1999); *Consistency Management and Cooperative Discipline* (Fashola & Slavin, 1998); *Promoting Alternative Thinking Strategies* (Greenberg, Domitrovich, & Bumbarger, 2000); *Seattle Social Development Project* (Hawkins, Catalano & Miller, 1991); and the *Bullying Prevention Program* (Olweus, 1993). All of these empirically supported programs target school- and classroom-level factors in order to influence students' behavior and academic performance

Box 4.1 Primary/Universal Programs and Strategies

1. School-wide positive behavioral interventions and supports (PBIS)
2. Safe and Responsive Schools (SRS) Project
3. Restorative practices
4. Social and emotional learning (SEL) programs
5. Character education programs
6. Effective classroom management strategies

(Bradshaw, Koth, Thornton, & Leaf, 2009). All of these programs have been discussed at length in other publications, and detailed information about each of them can be found on their respective Web sites.

The discussion of primary/universal programs and strategies in this chapter will highlight several empirically supported school-wide interventions designed to improve school climate and increase school connectedness, while being congruent with a more relationship-based, preventive model of school discipline. These primary/universal programs and strategies appear in Box 4.1.

School-Wide Positive Behavioral Interventions and Supports

Positive behavioral interventions and supports (PBIS) is a multitiered universal prevention strategy "that aims to modify the school environment by creating improved systems (e.g., discipline, reinforcement, data management) and procedures (e.g., office referral, reinforcement, training, leadership) that promote positive change in staff and student behaviors" (Bradshaw et al., 2009, p. 101). All stakeholders in the school community collaborate in establishing norms and behavioral expectations for the school, as well as create incentives for appropriate behavior, and constructive consequences and interventions for inappropriate behavior (Sullivan & Keeney, 2008). It has been estimated that PBIS is currently being implemented in over 7,500 schools in at least 44 states as well as several other countries (Sprague, 2008). Research studies have shown that PBIS was associated with several desirable school discipline outcomes, including a reduction in office discipline referrals (Taylor-Greene et al., 1997) and a reduction in suspensions (Horner, Sugai, Todd, & Lewis-Palmer, 2005), as well as a decrease in the time that administrators spent on discipline (Scott & Barrett, 2004). The PBIS strategy was also associated with improvements in school staff members' perceptions of their schools' organizational health (Bradshaw, Reinke, Brown, Bevans, & Leaf, 2008). The Technical Assistance Center on Positive Behavioral Interventions and Supports was established by the Office of Special Education Programs in the U.S. Department of Education to give schools capacity-building information and technical assistance for identifying, adapting, and sustaining effective school-wide disciplinary practices; it can be found at http://www.pbis.org/default.aspx.

Safe and Responsive Schools Project

The *Safe and Responsive Schools* (SRS) Project at the Indiana Education Policy Center is a model demonstration and technical assistance project that utilizes evidence-based practices and strategic planning to create a safe and responsive school climate. It also uses early identification and intervention, as well as effective responses to disruption and crises, by using alternatives to suspension and expulsion (Indiana University, 2002c). The SRS Project seeks to implement the best knowledge of school-wide behavior planning to develop and test a comprehensive model of systems change in school discipline emphasizing intervention at three levels (Indiana University, 2002c). Initial evaluation studies of this program have found significant reductions in school suspensions (Mayer & Leone, 2007). More information about the *Safe and Responsive Schools* Project can be found at their Web site at http://www.indiana.edu/~safeschl. A list of publications focusing on the *Safe and Responsive Schools* framework can be found at htttp://www.unl.edu/srs/publications.html.

Restorative Practices

Restorative practices refer to a number of programs, including *fairness committees, community circles, peer juries, peer courts, circles for teaching, conflict resolution*, as well as conferences that bring victims, offenders, and supporters together to address wrongdoing (Porter, 2007; Sullivan & Keeney, 2008). Restorative practices shift the burden of discipline from administrators to peers with the goal of repairing the harm that results from conflicts (Sullivan & Keeney, 2008). The most effective restorative programs are those that allow the student to have some input in resolving conflict in the most appropriate and fair way possible through the development of creative consequences that relate to the action (Sullivan & Keeney, 2008). A study of restorative practices in the United States, the United Kingdom, Canada, and New Zealand found that these

A New Model of School Discipline

practices resulted in a reduction in suspensions and detentions, and reduced stress for teachers (Porter, 2007). The authors of another reported that 66% of teachers stated that they felt that restorative practices were "effective to very effective" as a method of discipline (Sullivan & Keeney, 2008). The Web site for Safer Saner Schools, which contains information on helping improve school culture, classroom management, and student discipline through restorative practices, can be found at http://www.safersanerschools.org/index.html. The Web site for the International Institute for Restorative Practices can be found at http://www.iirp.org/

Peer mediation programs are a popular example of a restorative program in schools. Peer mediators are usually nominated by peers or teachers because they are respected and trusted by their peers and have demonstrated leadership and communication skills. Students come to mediation voluntarily, and peer mediators guide them through a process that moves from blaming each other to developing and committing to solutions that are acceptable to all parties (Indiana University, 2000b). Peer mediation programs have been found to be effective in improving student attitudes toward conflict, increasing understanding of nonviolent problem-solving methods, and enhancing communication skills (Ohio Commission on Dispute Resolution and Conflict Management, 1994). They have also reduced the number of school suspensions for fighting (Lam, 1989) and improved students' ability to manage conflicts (Deutsch et al., 1992). Another example of a restorative program is teen courts, also known as youth or peer courts. Teen courts are a relatively new concept in schools. Some schools have begun to use teen courts to administer school disciplinary actions. In these programs, the teen court determines the disciplinary consequences for violations of the school disciplinary codes. Potential benefits of teen courts include lower youth crime rates and and recidivism. The teen court program appears to be a promising alternative, although "more research on the impact of teen courts is needed (Indiana University, 2002a). More information about the youth courts and teen courts movement can be found in Peterson and Beres (2008).

Social and Emotional Learning Programs

A number of skills and competencies are necessary for students to be successful in school and throughout their lives. Students need to work effectively with students and adults, be able to effectively communicate and problem solve, and continue to try even in the face of discouragement or failure. Fortunately, these skills can be taught to diverse groups of students and the programs that teach these essential life skills are referred to as social and emotional learning (SEL) programs. According to the Collaborative for Academic, Social, and Emotional Learning (CASEL) (2007a), social and emotional skills include "recognizing and managing our emotions, developing caring and concern for others, establishing positive relationships, making responsible decisions, and handling challenging situations constructively and ethically. They are the skills that allow children to calm themselves when angry, make friends, resolve conflicts respectfully, and make ethical and safe choices" (p. 1). SEL programs should be planned, ongoing, systematic, and coordinated and should begin in preschool and continue through high school (Greenberg et al., 2003). A report by CASEL entitled *The Benefits of School-Based Social and Emotional Learning Programs: Highlights From a Forthcoming CASEL Report* (2007b) summarized key findings from a recent meta-analysis of 207 studies of SEL programs. These studies examined the impact of school-based SEL programs carried out by classroom teachers and other school staff. The authors of this report found that the overall group of SEL programs positively affected students in multiple areas, including enhanced skills, attitudes, and positive social behaviors as well as fewer conduct problems and lower levels of emotional distress. Another key finding from this meta-analysis is that maximum benefits are achieved when SEL programs are implemented as planned and school staff are adequately trained before implementing SEL programs. These programs appear to be one of the most successful youth-development interventions for racially and ethnically diverse students from urban, rural, and suburban settings that can be incorporated into routine educational practice during the regular school day and after school (Payton et al., 2008). The Web site for the CASEL, whose mission is to establish SEL as an essential part of education, can be found at http://www.casel.org/.

Character Education Programs

Character education encompasses curriculum and other activities at schools that promote civic virtue, the forms and rules of citizenship in a just society, and personal qualities that enable students to become productive and dependable citizens (London, 1987). A resurgence in character education among educators across the United States in recent years has resulted in a wide array of character education programs designed to teach moral virtue and conduct (Fallona & Richardson, 2006). The What Works Clearinghouse (WWC), established by the U.S. Department of Education's Institute of

Education Sciences in 2002, examined 93 studies of 41 different character education programs and found 18 studies of 13 programs that met their evidence standards. These standards related to reported or observed changes in student behavior, changes in students' knowledge, attitudes, and values related to ethical reasoning, and prosocial character and changes in academic achievement. A listing of these promising 13 character education programs and their effectiveness ratings across these three domains can be found at http://ies.ed.gov/ncee/wwc/reports/character_education/topic/tabfig.asp.

Effective Classroom Management Programs and Strategies

Classroom teachers have reported that they feel most underprepared in the area of classroom management (Pilarski, 1994). Specifically, teachers often lack the necessary skills to handle most minor problems in the classroom and address problems before they escalate into disciplinary referrals, with students being sent out of the classroom. A particular challenge facing teachers today is managing classrooms of ethnically, racially, and economically diverse students. Since many teacher training programs do not provide teachers with the skills needed to manage the behavior of students from diverse backgrounds (Rausch & Skiba, 2004), it appears that teachers are expected to perform tasks for which they have not been adequately prepared. A number of scholars and researchers have developed and discussed the critical elements of a culturally responsive pedagogy and the knowledge and skills needed by teachers to be "culturally responsive classroom managers." Weinstein, Curran, and Tomlinson-Clarke (2003) provide an overview of key elements of culturally responsive classroom managers. These are as follows:

1. Teachers are willing to reflect on the ways that classroom management decisions promote or obstruct students' access to learning.
2. Teachers recognize their biases and values and how these affect their interactions with students. For example, they ask, "Am I more patient and encouraging with some?" "Am I more likely to reprimand others?" "Do I expect African American and Latino children to be disruptive?" "Do I use hair style and dress to form stereotypical judgments of my students' character and academic potential?" "When students violate norms, do I recommend suspensions for students of color and parent conferences for students who are European American?"

3. Teachers strive to become knowledgeable about the cultures and communities in which their students live and acknowledge the legitimacy of different ways of speaking and interacting.
4. Teachers understand that the ultimate goal of classroom management is not to achieve compliance or control, but to provide all students with equitable opportunities for learning.

Several comprehensive classroom management programs and strategies designed for classrooms with general populations of students have received empirical support and been widely disseminated. These are as follows: the *Classroom Organization and Management Program* (COMP); the *Responsive Classroom* (RC); the *Good Behavior Game* (GBG); and the *Think Time Strategy* (TTS). The *Culture, Abilities, Resilience, and Effort* (CARE) Program is a promising curricula for working with ethnically, culturally, and economically diverse students. *The Classroom Organization and Management Program (COMP)* is a research-based professional development program designed to address both academic and social dimensions of learning within classrooms. Teachers completing COMP report significant positive changes in "students behavior, student achievement, and their personal satisfaction in teaching" (Classroom Organization and Management Program, 2004). More information about COMP can be found on their Web site at http://www.comp.org/#.

The Responsive Classroom (RC) program emphasizes social, emotional, and academic growth in elementary school classrooms and is based on the assumption that children require both academic and social-emotional skills. Evaluations of the RC program have been associated with higher student test scores, better social skills, and fewer problem behaviors and these findings held up across racially diverse subsamples (Northeast Foundation for Children Inc., n.d.). More information about the RC program can be found on their Web site at http://www.responsiveclassroom.org/about/aboutrc.html.

The Good Behavior Game (GBG) is a time-tested classroom strategy that utilizes positive peer pressure to shape students' behavior in the classroom. The GBG is "played" by dividing the class into two teams; a point is given to a team for any inappropriate behavior displayed by one of its members. The team with the fewest number of points at the conclusion of the GBG each day wins a group reward. If both teams keep their points below a preset level, then both teams share in the reward (Good Behavior Game, n.d.). The program was first tested in 1969 and several research articles have confirmed that the GBG is an effective means of increasing the rate of on-task behaviors while reducing disruptions in the classroom (Barrish, Saunders, & Wolf, 1969; Harris & Sherman, 1973; Medland & Stachnik, 1972). More information about the Good Behavior Game can be found on their Web site at http://www.interventioncentral.org/htmdocs/interventions/classroom/gbg.php.

The Think Time Strategy (TTS) was developed in response to research suggesting that attempts to stop disruptive classroom behavior sometimes aggravate the problem. It also was a reaction to a concern that many traditional classroom management systems or strategies that teachers use to deal with students who exhibit disruptive behaviors do not work well. The Think Time Strategy was designed as a universal prevention intervention for K–9 populations. The Think Time Strategy has five goals:

1. Enable teachers and students to cut off a negative social exchange or power struggle over disruptive behaviors
2. Eliminate coercive interaction patterns between teachers and students
3. Initiate a positive social exchange between teachers and students
4. Include students in the process of addressing their disruptive behavior
5. Decrease the variability in teachers' responses to disruptive behavior

The TTS requires that two or more teachers work together in a classroom to identify children exhibiting disruptive behavior. One teacher then moves a disruptive child to a distraction-free environment, gives the child time to think about his or her behavior, and then discusses the behavior with the child before returning the child to his or her classroom (U.S. Department of Education, 2001). Evaluation results demonstrated positive effects of TTS for the Severely Emotionally Disturbed (SED) population. A study involving three female and 22 male students in grades one through six showed that the average number of critical events (e.g., verbal and physical aggression) decreased by 77% weekly across all three classrooms and that two of the three classrooms continued to show decreases in the number of critical events during follow-up. In addition, the average duration of estimated on-task time that students spent increased by 34% weekly across all three classrooms, and all three classrooms continued to demonstrate increases in on-task performance during follow-up (U.S. Department of Education, 2001). More information about *The Think Time Strategy* can be found on the Promising Practices Network Web site at http://www.promisingpractices.net/program.asp?programid=258.

Unfortunately, there is little empirical research on the effectiveness of specific programs designed to equip teachers with the necessary knowledge and skills to become culturally responsive classroom managers. One of the more promising curricula is the National Education Association's CARE Program Curriculum. The acronym *CARE* stands for "culture, abilities, resilience, and effort." As we learn about the cultures that students bring to school, and how to connect these cultures to what students learn, educators must also "learn about the culture that permeates school and how it advantages or disadvantages certain students . . . as educators working together to make these changes, we are not only advancing our profession, we are advancing the very goals of social justice . . ." (National Education Association, 2005). The CARE program was developed through the collaborative efforts of teachers, education support professionals, researchers, community advocates, parents, and practitioners.

Proven and Promising Secondary/Targeted Programs and Strategies

Secondary/targeted programs and strategies target behaviorally at-risk students to keep minor behavior problems and difficulties from developing into more serious ones. They reflect and support a relationship-based model of school discipline. The secondary/targeted programs and strategies discussed in this chapter appear in Box 4.2.

Box 4.2 Secondary/Targeted Programs and Strategies

- School-based mentoring programs
- In-school suspension programs
- Anger management training
- School transition programs
- Threat assessment/early warning signs and screening

A New Model of School Discipline

School-Based Mentoring Programs

School-based mentoring (SBM) is a rapidly expanding form of mentoring. In 2005, almost 870,000 adults were mentoring children in schools as part of a formal program (Herrera, Grossman, Kauh, Feldman, & McMaken, 2007). Mentors may be recruited formally or informally from corporations or local businesses, professional organizations, faith communities, law enforcement, college faculties, or retirement communities. Teachers and counselors can also be assigned as mentors to students (McPartland & Slavin, 1990). Since African-American and Hispanic males are disproportionately at-risk of being suspended or expelled, it is particularly important that African-American and Hispanic males be recruited as mentors. A study of school-based mentoring programs reported that, relative to their nonmentored peers, mentees showed improvements in serious school infractions (including visits to the principal's office, fighting, and suspensions), overall academic performance, and skipping school (Herrera et al., 2007). Mentees also reported that the school-based mentoring program provided them with "someone they look up to and talk to about personal problems, who cares about what happens to them and influences the choices they make" (Herrera et al., 2007, p. iv). This same study also found that longer matches and closer relationships between mentors and mentees were associated with stronger impacts. A number of publications focusing on school-based mentoring programs can be found at the Northwest Regional Educational Laboratory's National Mentoring Center's Web site at http://www.nwrel.org/mentoring/links_school.php.

In-School Suspension Programs

In-school suspension (ISS) programs began proliferating in the 1970s as an alternative to out-of-school suspensions by punishing a student but not requiring the misbehaving student to miss classes (Center for Mental Health in Schools at UCLA, 2005). While ISS programs are a desirable alternative to out-of-school suspensions, poorly conceived ISS programs are little more than "holding tanks" and often serve as brief stops on the way to out-of-school suspension (Delisio, 2003; Sanders, 2001). Many poorly conceived ISS programs emphasize keeping students busy with school work and isolating them from other students, but they fail to address and modify the behaviors that resulted in the student being assigned to ISS. As a result, students often return to their classrooms with the same, or worse, behaviors and end up in ISS on a repeated basis or get suspended out of school (Delisio, 2003).

The most effective in-school suspension programs focus on improving student behavior by including counseling components and conflict resolution strategies (Ingersoll & Le Boeuf, 1997). One of the few in-school suspension programs that emphasizes behavioral change and that has undergone an evaluation is the *On-campus Intervention Program (OCIP)*. According to Family Resources (2001), the *OCIP* provides counseling to help the students change their disruptive behavior and explore alternatives. In the short term, OCIP's goal is to modify behavior. Its long-term goal is to improve the learning environment in classrooms by reducing disruptions. Students are assigned to OCIP at the discretion of the building principal. The program is voluntary; parents of students referred for suspension are given the choice for their child to attend OCIP or serve out his or her out-of-school suspension. There is evidence that the OCIP is effective in modifying student behaviors. Specifically, 72% of students referred to OCIP in middle schools and 76% of students referred to OCIP in high school did not receive subsequent referrals to the OCIP program. In addition, in those schools where OCIP was fully implemented, there was a 49% reduction in out-of-school suspensions in middle schools and 34% reduction in out-of-school suspensions in high schools (Family Resources, 2001).

Anger Management Training

School-based anger management interventions have proliferated in recent years. Rather than a "one-size-fits-all" approach, effective anger management programs target specific anger-related problems, including chronically high levels of angry feelings, hostile attitudes toward others, and the tendency to express anger in destructive or hurtful ways (Smith, 2008). The most effective interventions employ cognitive-behavioral techniques, including anger regulation and control, problem solving to learn alternatives to aggression as an expression of anger, and cognitive restructuring to change maladaptive thought processes (Smith, 2008). Anger management training appears most useful in reducing incidents of spontaneous or "reactive" aggression as opposed to more deliberate, intentional, or "proactive" acts of aggression (Smith, 2008). Anger management programs delivered in school settings have the most empirical support for reducing angry feelings experienced at school as well as negative expression of these feelings through destructive and aggressive behaviors (Smith, 2008). Students trained in anger management have been found to decrease their disruptive and aggressive behaviors both at home and in the classroom, and to display greater self-control (Feindler,

Marriot, & Iwata, 1984). Long-term benefits of anger management training, however, still need to be proven.

School Transition Programs

It is important to recognize that many students will have a difficult time with the transition from elementary to middle school and the transition from middle to high school. Elias (2001) describes a number of potential challenges facing students as they transition into middle school: finding their way around a strange building, finding and opening a locker for the first time, eating in a larger cafeteria, and changing clothes in a crowded locker room. Students must also find and connect with new friends, deal with emerging feelings about members of the opposite sex, and may experience bullying or harassment from older students. Some students may have conflicts with their teachers and be disciplined. A reason for many behavioral problems in middle school is the fact that many students are not well prepared for the academic demands. To help ease the transition from elementary to middle school, Elias (2001) offers a number of proactive strategies that can be implemented by middle school administrators:

- Make sure that each incoming student has an older "buddy" who initiates contact before the beginning of the school year and provides ongoing support.
- Teach middle school survival skills to students. These skills should include the following: how to respond to peer pressure; how to organize time and resources for classwork and homework; understanding and addressing the varying expectations of teachers in different subject areas; and accomplishing such basic tasks as studying, taking notes, and taking tests.
- Schedule early and periodic individual or group counseling visits for new students so that they do not have to take the initiative in seeking help if they are having problems.

The move from middle school to high school is another major and important transition for many students. As before, many of these changes are related to getting used to a new school setting, more demanding instructional content and academic standards, changes in one's role and status, as well as new interpersonal relationships (School Mental Health Project, n.d.). The authors of this report offer a number of interventions that can be implemented by school administrators to help ease the transition into ninth grade:

- Offer a transition course in eighth grade and use opportunities throughout the school day to enhance specific knowledge, skills, and attitudes related to the upcoming transition into high school.
- Connect eighth graders to ninth grade *peer buddies* during the last month before the transition or at least from the first day in ninth grade. Peer buddies are trained to orient, welcome, and introduce the newcomer to peers and activities during the first few weeks of transition as well as to provide social support.
- An individual transition plan, with specific tasks and objectives, can be developed for those students identified as likely to have difficulty with the transition. These programs need to be implemented no later than the middle of eighth grade.
- Personalized transition supports and assistance should be provided to students who do not appear to be making a successful transition into ninth grade (based on teacher reports).

Cauley and Jovanovich (2006) recommend that all transition programs should also take into account the unique needs of minority students and low-income students. Effective transition programs should extend beyond the school building to help students handle problems originating at home or in their community.

A program that targets students in transition from elementary and middle schools in large urban areas with multiple feeders serving predominantly non-White lower income youths is the *School Transitional Environmental Program* (STEP). Students in STEP are assigned to homerooms in which all classmates are STEP participants, and they are enrolled in the same core classes to help develop stable peer groups and enhance participants' familiarity with the school. Homeroom teachers act as administrators and guidance counselors, providing class schedule assistance, academic counseling in school, and counseling in school for personal problems. Teachers also explain the project to parents and notify them of student absences (The

Sourcebook of Drug and Violence Prevention Programs for Children and Adolescents, 2008). An evaluation of the STEP program with lower risk students in junior high demonstrated that STEP students, compared with control students, showed significantly lower levels of school transition stress and better adjustment on measures of school, family, general self-esteem, depression, anxiety, and delinquent behavior, and higher levels of academic expectations. Teachers in the STEP schools reported that their students had better classroom adjustment behavior and fewer problem behaviors (The Sourcebook of Drug and Violence Prevention Programs for Children and Adolescents, 2008).

Threat Assessment/Early Warning Signs and Screening

Students at risk for violence often engage in visible minor behavior problems, such as aggression and poor school attitude, before progressing to more violent acts (Mihalic, & Grotpeter, 1997). Therefore, an essential component of any comprehensive, preventive school discipline program is the implementation of a system designed to identify students who may be at risk for committing violent acts and delineating the actions to be taken in response to these potential threats. In response to this need, a number of screening measures that list early warning signs based on valid and reliable research findings have been developed. These measures provide schools with a valuable tool for early identification of students in need and a method for identifying at-risk students before they escalate into disruption or violence (Walker & Severson, 1992). One commercially available school-wide screening measure is the *Systematic Screening for Behavioral Disorders. Early Warning, Timely Response: A Guide to Safe Schools.* This measure highlights early and imminent warning signs and procedures for developing appropriate responses to warning signs. It also cautions that none of its recommended policies or procedures should be used to harm or label children (Dwyer, Osher, & Warger, 1998). Schools and families should be careful not to overreact to a single sign; students at-risk for serious aggression or violence typically exhibit more than one warning sign (Dwyer, Osher, & Warger, 1998). Developmental issues should also be a part of any risk assessment. For example, a warning sign at one grade level may be more typical of students at another grade level (Dwyer, Osher, & Warger, 1998). Sprague and Walker (2000) also discuss a number of strategies that can be used with middle school students to identify students at high risk of committing violent and aggressive acts as well as important cautions about the use of such strategies. They stated:

> Generally, warning signs of their prior exposure to environmental risks are clearly in evidence early on in the lives and school careers of antisocial children and youth. These signs are reflected in the behavioral characteristics of many at-risk children at the point of school entry and become elaborated during the elementary school years. These warning signs vary substantially in terms of how well they predict or are associated with juvenile violence; all should be of serious concern, however. The more of these signs a student manifests, the greater the risk, and the greater the urgency for appropriate intervention.

The authors of Early Identification and Intervention (Indiana University, 2000a) outline several essential components that should be included in any building- or district-specific policy for identifying students who may be at-risk for committing violent acts:

- *Reporting of threats by students.* Students need to be provided with information about what constitutes a reportable threat or warning sign, and students must be assured they will be protected from retribution for making a report.
- *Taking threats seriously.* Teachers and parents need to be encouraged to pass along all reports to school administration, and perhaps local law enforcement. If there is no response to a serious report, both reporters and their peers will be less likely to communicate future incidents.
- *Preplanned responses.* All policies regarding the identification of students who may be at risk for committing violent acts should be written down and communicated to all staff in advance, to avoid panic in a threat situation.
- *Relationships with local law enforcement and mental health agencies.* A well-established relationship with the local police department and mental health agencies that allows clear and open communication regarding any threat is extremely helpful. For example, the following question needs to be answered ahead of time: Who will make the report, and to whom?

Box 4.3 Tertiary/Remedial Programs and Strategies

- Functional behavioral assessment
- System of care/wraparound approaches
- Multi-systemic therapy (MST)
- Treatment foster care
- Identifying students with emotional disturbance (ED)

Proven and Promising Tertiary/Remedial Programs and Strategies

Tertiary/remedial programs and strategies are designed for students who do not respond to a secondary/targeted intervention and require more powerful and intensive interventions. These programs and strategies "seek to minimize the future damage of aggression to the child and others" (Skiba & Rausch, 2006, p. 1079). The tertiary/remedial programs and strategies discussed in this chapter appear in Box 4.3.

Functional Behavioral Assessment

An important support for students with emotional disabilities or severe behavior problems is the practice of identifying the purpose of a behavior before selecting and applying an intervention. This is the foundation of the practice known as functional behavioral assessment (FBA; Epstein, Atkins, Cullinan, Kutash, & Weaver, 2008). Epstein, Atkins, Cullinan, Kutash, and Weaver (2008) provided a detailed description of the FBA process:

> A functional behavioral assessment identifies and measures a specific problem behavior by describing and analyzing the student's interactions in his [or her] environment to understand variables that contribute to the occurrence of the misbehavior. There is no standard set of resources and procedures to conduct a functional behavioral assessment, but often it includes a variety of indirect assessments (for example, teacher interviews, parent interviews, or school records review), direct assessments (such as classroom observations or standardized behavior checklists), and data analysis conducted by the school psychologist or other behavioral experts to determine whether there are patterns associated with the behavior. (p. 15)

For a detailed overview of methods and procedures to conduct a functional behavioral assessment, visit the Center for Effective Collaboration and Practice Web site at http://cecp.air.org/fba/.

System of Care/Wraparound Approach

System of care and wraparound approaches bring together education, mental health, juvenile justice, and other community youth-serving agencies to collaborate and develop integrated services and additional resources to schools to address the most serious and challenging behaviors (Skiba & Rausch, 2006). In wraparound, a team (e.g., families, friends, relatives, professionals from schools, mental health, child welfare, and juvenile justice) works to identify the underlying needs, interests, and limitations of families and service providers, and to develop a comprehensive plan that addresses these interests using natural, community supports wherever possible (Burchard, 2000; Eber, Nelson, & Miles, 1997). These teams also "inventory, coordinate, and, if necessary, create supports, services, and interventions to address agreed upon needs of the youth and primary caregivers (i.e. families, teachers) across home, school, and community" (Indiana University, 2002b). The unique needs in the life domains of safety, medical, social, psychological, basic needs, and living environment drive the planning process, and the family has a strong voice in creating and implementing the plan. The plan combines natural supports (e.g., child care, transportation, mentors, parent-to-parent support) with more traditional interventions (e.g., positive behavior interventions, teaching social skills, reading instruction, therapy) (Indiana University, 2002b). While there is not a broad base of research support for wraparound, some studies have reported improved behavioral, academic, social, and postschool adjustment indicators for children involved with wraparound. One of the central arguments used to promote wraparound is that service in the community is less costly than service in a residential treatment center (Indiana University, 2002b).

Multisystemic Therapy

Multisystemic therapy (MST) is a research-supported, cost-effective, intensive family- and community-based treatment for youth with serious behavioral problems. Multisystemic therapy uses a home-based, family preservation model of service delivery to address factors associated with delinquency across those systems (i.e., family, peers, school, neighborhood) in the youth's natural environment (Henggeler, Schoenwald, Borduin, Rowland, & Cunningham, 1998). One of the major goals of MST is to prevent out-of-home placements for youth through the provision of intensive, family-based supports, services, and intervention. Key features of the MST include intensive supervision, interagency collaboration, and consultation (MST Services, 2007). *Multisystemic therapy* is particularly appropriate for use with antisocial youth who are early starters and more likely to become recidivists (Moffitt, 1994). *Multisystemic therapy* is included in the Blueprint Series of scientifically validated, violence prevention programs established by the Center for the Study and Prevention of Violence and is a thoroughly researched intervention model that works effectively for the most severely involved, at-risk adolescents (see Schoenwald et al., 2000). Studies with violent and chronic juvenile offenders showed that MST reduced long-term rates of rearrest by 25% to 70% compared with control groups. Furthermore, studies with long-term follow-ups showed that MST reduced days in out-of-home placements by 47% to 64% compared with control groups (MST Services, n.d.). Research on the effectiveness of MST can be found at http://www.mstservices.com/research_on_effectiveness.php.

Treatment Foster Care

Treatment foster care is an intensive, family-focused intervention designed for youth whose delinquency is so serious and chronic that they are no longer permitted to live at home (Dwyer & Osher, 2000). Like MST, it includes every major aspect of a youth's life in the intervention (i.e., individual, family, peers, and school). The treatment foster care model is based on the assumption that normal parenting resources are profoundly diminished by the challenges of living with a youth who exhibits serious antisocial behavior (Dwyer & Osher, 2000). Treatment foster care families are recruited for their willingness to act as treatment agents and their ability to provide a nurturing family environment. They provide youths with a structured daily living environment with close supervision, clear rules, and enforcement of limits (Dwyer & Osher, 2000).

Identifying Students With Emotional Disturbance (ED)

It has been estimated that 4 to 6 million children and youth have emotional disturbance (ED) (Housewright, 1999; Quindlen, 1999). However, only 1% are identified by schools as ED and only two-thirds of those receive any type of mental health treatment (Housewright, 1999; Quindlen, 1999). Consequently, it is important for schools to evaluate whether a student with severe behavior problems is eligible for special education services under IDEA. If a student is found to be eligible due to having an emotional disturbance, interventions and

---

supports must be incorporated into the student's individualized education plan (IEP). As noted by Dwyer and Osher (2000):

> Special education eligibility under IDEA includes the designation of emotional disturbance. In general, under the federal definition, this designation includes children and youth demonstrating unsatisfactory personal relationships with peers and teachers and who have inappropriate types of behaviors or feelings under normal circumstances. For children who are eligible under IDEA, and whose behavior interferes with their learning or the learning of others, the IEP Team must consider, if appropriate, positive behavioral interventions, strategies, and supports to address that behavior...It is important to note that positive behavioral interventions and supports, like other services provided to students with disabilities, can be implemented in the regular education classroom. (p. 32)

Summary

Any comprehensive program designed to improve school climates and reduce student behavior problems must be as effective, pragmatic, and cost efficient as possible.Unfortunately, a number of widely used school security measures have not been empirically supported in relation to improving school climate or reducing student behavior problems. It is also important to address problems in the way in which school-level and state-wide discipline data are currently collected and reported to the general public.

In schools, three distinct groups of students lie along a risk continuum, and differing types of intervention should be provided to groups of students along this continuum of need, at each of three intervention levels (i.e., primary/universal, secondary/targeted, and tertiary/remedial). A broad array of proven and promising programs and strategies at each of these three intervention levels have been developed and implemented across the United States to reduce discipline problems and improve school climate. Rather than a one-size-fits-all, prescribed model, the wide array of empirically supported programs and strategies designed allows individual school districts to meet their unique needs in the most effective, pragmatic, and cost-efficient manner possible.

5

■ ■ ■

The Hard Part: Making Organizational Changes in Schools

Now comes the hard part. The challenges involved in moving from a traditional model of school discipline to a relationship-based model of discipline should not be underestimated. In this final chapter, I document the major challenges in making school-wide organizational changes with a particular focus on those unique obstacles in changing school discipline practices. Following this, I present a five-stage strategic planning process that is designed to move from a traditional, punitive model of school discipline to a preventive, relationship-based model of discipline that reflects the comprehensive, preventive, multitiered framework I discussed in Chapters 3 and 4. I conclude this final chapter with a discussion of several additional key points to consider in making significant systemic changes in schools.

Why Is Organizational Change So Difficult to Achieve in Schools?

We must first acknowledge that making any type of substantive organizational change is very difficult and will bring about much resistance. It has been estimated that one-third to two-thirds of major change initiatives fail (Beer & Nohria, 2000). Why is there such a high failure rate? There are a number of personal reasons as well as systemic reasons. For example, a number of people resist any type of change effort because new ways of doing things make them uncomfortable and anxious (Greene, 2008). Some school personnel people would prefer to keep doing things the same way despite that fact that what they are currently doing may not be working. School personnel often view calls for change as personal criticism, triggering a defensive reaction and resistance (Annie E. Casey Foundation, 1995). This personal resistance to change can be played out passively or actively. It has been estimated that about 20% of any school staff are traditional, steadfast resisters who often reject change completely (Gilley, Gilley, & McMillan, 2009). These teachers have been described as disengaged and undermotivated, but unwilling or unable to leave their current position (Cherniss & Adler, 2000). Another reason that some people may resist change is that they are "initiative weary" and view any new program as the "latest fad" that will fade away as others have in the past. This view has been also been referred to as "project mentality" or "projectitis," and this perception will often marginalize new change initiatives (Adelman & Taylor, 2007).

There are also systemic reasons why new program initiatives fail. First and foremost, organizational change does not just involve the implementation of new programs; it involves changing the culture and climate of a school. A school's *culture* is the socially shared and transmitted knowledge of what is and what ought to be (e.g., how should people behave toward one another, what norms and beliefs should be shared by everyone) (Hamilton & Richardson, 1995). Closely related to culture is the concept of *climate,* which has been defined as the "heart and soul of a school. It is about the essence of a school that leads a child, a teacher, an administrator, or a staff member to love the school and to look forward to being at their school each day" (Freiberg & Stein, 1999, p. 11). Since systemic change involves a "cultural shift in institutionalized values (i.e., reculturalization), the greater the distance and dissonance between the current culture of schools and intended school improvements, the more difficult it is to successfully accomplish major systemic changes" (Adelman & Taylor, 2007, p. 56).

Another reason that change efforts often fail has to do with the change agents themselves. Unfortunately, persons who are expected to act as change agents often lack specific training in facilitating major systemic changes (Adelman & Taylor, 2007). There is evidence that even some change agents themselves are resistant to new change initiatives (Ford, Ford, & D'Amelio, 2008). Beyond these general concerns and barriers, attempts to change the traditional discipline system of a school or school district introduce a number of unique challenges and obstacles.

Why Is It So Difficult to Change Traditional Discipline Practices in Schools?

The challenge to move from a traditional model of discipline to a relationship-based model of discipline within a school community cannot be overestimated. These types of comprehensive changes are very difficult and take an extraordinary amount of time and energy (Annie E. Casey Foundation, 1995). There are a number of reasons for this. First of all, it is important to acknowledge that the current traditional punitive model of discipline is deeply embedded in the culture and climate of the vast majority of U.S. public schools. Fundamental changes in school discipline policies and procedures will necessarily invoke anxiety and resistance among some school personnel because they necessitate a major cultural shift. Some teachers may resist new discipline strategies that involve teaching and positive feedback because these strategies take significantly more time than simple punishment (Parker-Pope, 2008). A shift to a relationship-based model of discipline will also require the development of warm relationships with students, and some teachers may be unable, as a result of personality and temperament, to develop these types of nurturing relationships (Watson & Battistich, 2006). Some teachers may also be overwhelmed by stressful working conditions without much collegial support and adopt survival mechanisms to get them through the school day, which preclude the development of caring relationships with students (Milner, 2006). Some teachers and administrators may hold the belief that any new discipline approach will make their school less safe (Greene, 2008).

It must also be recognized that some teachers and administrators may resist changing current discipline practices because they do not want to change the existing power relationships in schools (Sarason, 1990). Changing from a traditional top-down model of discipline to a more relationship-based model of discipline will challenge these power relationships in significant ways. For example, some teachers will resist any effort to change how they currently manage their classrooms (Morrison, Blood, & Thorsborne, 2005) because they feel that "they are already doing a good job with their challenging students and don't see the need to change course, or may be somewhat resentful of anyone's efforts to alter what they do in their classrooms" (Greene, 2008, pp. 229–230). Moreover, most school principals have considerable authority and discretion in how they deal with discipline matters within their own school building, and their personal discipline philosophy largely determines how disciplinary policies are carried out

(Browne, 2003). For example, it has been shown that principals with more favorable attitudes toward excluding students from school had higher suspension rates compared with schools with principals who emphasized less punitive outcomes (Rausch & Skiba, 2004). It goes without saying that a change to a relationship-based model of discipline will be viewed as a threat to some principals in terms of how they view their authority and their personal philosophy of discipline.

Another important systemic barrier is the "waiting for failure" approach that schools have historically taken in dealing with behavior problems. Schools have historically done little to prevent problems or intervene early (Center for Mental Health Services in Schools at UCLA, n.d.a). In addition, as I noted in Chapter 3, many school administrators and teachers view students' behavioral problems as disturbances within the child and, therefore, limit their interventions to "fixing the child" rather than intervening at multiple levels in multiple ways.

In essence, systemic change in schools involves "monumental effort, unusual resourcefulness, and strong leadership of key individuals or groups" (Hatch, 2000, p. 581). While the obstacles and challenges to changing school discipline practices may appear to be insurmountable, much has been learned over the past several decades about how to anticipate and overcome these obstacles and barriers through a systematic planning process referred to as strategic planning for organizational change.

Strategic Planning for Organizational Change

Strategic planning for organizational change is a systematic process that provides a framework and map for how to get from "here to there" by considering both internal and external strengths, weaknesses, threats, and opportunities (Adelman & Taylor, 2007; Knoff, 2002). A number of authors have developed very useful frameworks for thinking about, implementing, and sustaining systemic changes in a school or school district. Adelman and Taylor (2007) describe this process as consisting of four overlapping phases:

1. *Creating readiness*—increasing a climate/culture for change through enhancing the motivation and capability of a critical mass of stakeholders
2. *Initial implementation*—carrying out change in stages using a well-designed infrastructure to provide guidance and support

3. *Institutionalization*—ensuring there is an infrastructure to maintain and enhance productive changes

4. *Ongoing evolution and creative renewal*—using mechanisms to improve quality and provide continuing support in ways that enable stakeholders to become a community of learners who creatively pursue renewal. (p. 61)

Skiba, Ritter, Simmons, Peterson, and Miller (2006) present a four-stage strategic planning process developed by the Safe and Responsive Schools Project. These stages are as follows:

1. Team formation
2. Needs assessment
3. Best practices review
4. Strategic planning

Morrison, Blood, and Thorsborne (2005) discuss a five-stage, long-term strategic approach specifically designed to change the traditional culture of discipline in Australian schools. Their framework is very useful because it explicitly reflects the comprehensive, preventive, multitiered framework for moving to a new paradigm of school discipline (as discussed in Chapters 3 and 4). It also sets a realistic timeline for accomplishing activities within each stage. These stages are as follows:

1. *Gaining commitment:* Capturing hearts and minds
2. *Developing a shared vision:* Knowing where we are going and why
3. *Developing responsive and effective practice:* Changing how we do things around here
4. *Developing a whole-school approach:* Putting it all together
5. *Developing professional relationships:* Walking the talk with each other

Morrison, Blood, and Thorsborne also state that their five stages are "recursive rather than linear" with the fifth stage running concurrently with all other stages (p. 345).

I will now describe a five-stage strategic planning process designed to move a school or school district from a traditional, punitive model of discipline to a relationship-based model of discipline. This five-stage strategic planning process acknowledges and directly addresses the obstacles and barriers discussed earlier in this chapter. In addition to borrowing heavily from the works of Adelman and Taylor (2007), Skiba, Ritter, Simmons, Peterson, and Miller (2006), and Morrison, Blood, and Thorsborne (2005) discussed above, my discussion also incorporates key points from the works of Knoff (2002); Annie E. Casey Foundation (1995); Everson (1995); Everhart and Wandersman (2000); Elias, Zins, Graczyk, and Weissberg (2003); and the Center for Mental Health in Schools at UCLA (2006, 2007).

Before discussing the stages involved in this change process, it is important to understand who leads and guides this process. Schools often bring in specially trained change agents, called *organization facilitators*, to guide this strategic change process (Adelman & Taylor, 1997; Center for Mental Health in Schools at UCLA, 2006). However, it is important to remember that any outside catalyst, such as organization facilitators, should be "limited partners" and not owners of the change process. Local "buy-in" is critical in implementing and sustaining organizational change (Annie E. Casey Foundation, 1995).

According to the Center for Mental Health Services in School at UCLA (n.d.b), the organization facilitator is someone who understands "the fundamental concerns underlying the need for change, the nature and scope of the innovation to be implemented ... [and] how to work with stakeholders as they rethink and rework their policies, interventions, infrastructure, and institutional culture" (p. 6). The major tasks of the organization facilitator revolve around planning, facilitating, and assisting school sites as they adopt/adapt, implement, and institutionalize systemic change efforts. The Center Report, entitled *Organization Facilitators: A Key Change Agent for Systemic School and Community Changes,* is a valuable reference containing detailed information about the roles and functions of organization facilitators (Center for Mental Health Services in School, n.d., p. 6).

Stage 1: Assessing Readiness and Capacity for Change

The first stage involves a significant amount of preplanning and assessment with a particular focus on assessing a school's or school district's *readiness* and *capacity* for organizational change. A major reason so many organizational change efforts are not successful is because sufficient time and attention were not given to the *readiness* and *capacity* for change among a critical mass of stakeholders, especially principals and teachers (Annie E. Casey Foundation, 1995; Elias et al., 2003; Sugai & Horner, 1999). For example, Payne, Gottfredson, and Gottfredson (2006) found significant associations between principal support and organizational capacity and the implementation quality of school-based prevention programs. In essence, change agents must *attend to existing organizational factors before embarking on significant systemic change efforts.*

During this initial stage, it is important to learn as much as possible about the organizational structure and personnel, including formal and informal rules and norms, policies and procedures, and organizational history and environment. This *needs assessment* is a critical step because schools will differ in their readiness to restructure their disciplinary system (Skiba et al., 2006). It is important that the planned changes match the areas that need changing, and that the planned changes are linked to stated goals of schools or school districts. One method for obtaining a thorough understanding of these organizational aspects of the school is through a *mapping process*. This mapping process should include a detailed examination of the school's (or school district's) discipline polices and practices. It can also be used to assess a school's willingness to establish mechanisms and processes that facilitate change efforts. For a detailed description of the mapping process as well as available tools that can be used to conduct a thorough mapping process in a school, see the Center for Mental Health in Schools at UCLA (2006) publication *A Technical Aid Packet on Resource Mapping and Management to Address Barriers to Learning: An Intervention for Systemic Change.*

Stage 2: Commitment to the Change Process: Making a Compelling Case for Change

This stage involves seeking out and involving key stakeholders in the change process. To begin with, school administrators must be "onboard" and provide consistent support; after all, they are the gatekeepers to all change processes within their school, including disciplinary matters. While administrators "may not be onboard initially, a critical number will need to come onboard at some point for the process to be sustainable" (Morrison et al., 2005, p. 347). In addition, teachers, parents, and students should be sought out and involved. This essential buy-in process has been aptly described by Morrison et al. (2005) as "capturing hearts and minds." In other words, a systems change effort must excite the individuals it needs to engage.

A compelling case must be made that the current discipline system is flawed and fundamental change is required to fix it; "without a profound loyalty to this proposition, it is difficult to prevent a difficult reform initiative from eroding into just another service 'project'" (Annie E. Casey Foundation, 1995, p. 12).

Some school personnel will become excited and be moved to action through the telling of stories. Denning (2005, 2007) explains how *storytelling* can be used to catalyze action in modern change-resistant organizations. According to Denning, resistance is inevitable when a bold new idea is presented; the challenge is how to turn this resistance into enthusiasm. Rather than explaining a new complicated and multidimensional idea, which can often kill enthusiasm even before it is implemented, Denning argues that telling a story can often help school personnel to think about a different kind of future both for the school as an organization and themselves as individuals. While some in the school will be moved by storytelling, others will be moved by the presentation of hard quantitative data (i.e., numbers of office referrals, suspensions, expulsions, and student attendance records) that provide empirical evidence that there are discipline problems in their school. The telling of stories, combined with the sharing of hard data, can be utilized to challenge current disciplinary practices and make a strong and compelling case for buy-in and ownership of and commitment to this change effort. Change agents cannot wait for a complete buy-in before taking action because ownership of a new program grows over time. In other words, when a change initiative begins, "it may signal not the beginning of change, but, at best, the beginning of readiness for change" (Elias et al., 2003).

Additional efforts to capture hearts and minds involve addressing the concerns that educators have about change, as discussed earlier in this chapter (e.g., "projectitis," any new discipline approach will make their school less safe, etc.,) in a direct, honest, and empathic manner because "adults, just like kids, are more likely to participate in solving problems when they feel that their concerns aren't being disregarded" (Greene, 2008, pp. 229–230). It is important to remember that acknowledging and addressing the emotional impact of change is as important as putting new structure and practices in place (Morrison et al., 2005).

It is also important to be aware that different groups of individuals in any school will have various attitudes and feelings about change efforts (Gilley et al., 2009) that will impact the strategies and timing of any buy-in efforts. As discussed earlier, approximately 20% of staff within every school will resist and undermine any change efforts in a school. It is important not to waste

---

A New Model of School Discipline

energy trying to engage this group; the best way to deal with them is to agree to disagree with them and try to neutralize their negative influence on other groups within the school as much as possible. One effective way to neutralize their influence is to enlist the support and enthusiasm of those individuals who thrive on change. Other groups of individuals who should be targeted early for buy-in efforts are those who seek challenges and generally like change as well as those who prefer to wait and see and observe the impact of change on others prior to making a deliberate decision to change themselves. A more difficult group to "capture" are those individuals who are skeptical, sometimes suspicious of change, and support change only as a last resort. One way of getting buy-in from those most skeptical of change is to make sure that change efforts include action, not just talk, early in the process and to be able to answer the questions, What is in this change for me? and How will I benefit from this change?

Stage 3: Collaborative Groups: Developing and Articulating a Shared Vision

An important task in this stage is to develop and articulate a clear, shared vision for the work to be accomplished and to develop outcomes aligned with this shared vision. If educational innovations lack this type of clarity, there will be less motivation to carry them out (Elias et al., 2003). To carry out this task in a strategic manner, collaborative groups consisting of district- and building-level school personnel, parents, and community leaders should be formed (Knoff, 2002). This is because implementing and sustaining systemic changes in schools can be accomplished much more effectively by committed and energized collaborative groups of individuals, rather than individuals working in isolation. These collaborative groups should include the following members of the school community: principal or assistant principal, school psychologist, counselor, school nurse, school social worker, behavioral specialist, special education teacher, and student representation. The following community stakeholders should also be involved in these collaborative groups: attorneys, judges, and probation officers; business leaders, clergy, and other representatives of the faith community; college or university faculty; family agency and family resource center staff; interest group representatives and grassroots community organization members; law enforcement personnel; local advisory board members; local officials, including school board members and representatives from special commissions;

mental health and child welfare personnel; parent group leaders, such as Parent–Teacher Association (PTA) officers; advocacy group leaders; physicians and nurses; recreational, cultural, and arts organizations staff; school public relations officers; youth workers and volunteers; other influential community members; and parents. As more and more individuals and stakeholders come onboard, a continual process of "widening the lens" occurs.

To accomplish work in as efficient a manner as possible, clear roles should be delineated for all members of these collaborative groups. Frank and respectful communication should be an ongoing aspect of the collaborative group process. An effective way of improving communication among members of collaborative groups is to develop a common language. For example, every team member should understand the meanings and definitions of all terms and concepts used, and acronyms should be explained.

Collaborative team members should establish evaluation processes and accountability procedures. It is difficult to sustain new practices and easy to slip back into old habits, particularly when something does not work for the first time. A person's beliefs and practices must change in order to produce successful results. Therefore, it is important to acknowledge and reinforce the changes that occur along the way by establishing interim benchmarks (e.g., short-, medium-, and long-term milestones). Measures, such as reducing suspensions or office referrals by 10%, become markers for schools to know when they are accomplishing their goals. If something does not work, it is important to regroup and try another strategy.

There are a number of systemic and institutional barriers to working collaboratively across groups of individuals. Dryfoos (1994) has aptly described collaboration as "an unnatural act between nonconsenting adults." For example, most school cultures do not support collaborative activities; teachers work in isolation in many schools; differing orientations and values and ethics among various group members can often lead to conflict and distrust; much time is spent defending one's turf; and team members often perceive other team members as less qualified (Hooper-Briar & Lawson, 1994; Knoff, 2002). It must be acknowledged that true collaboration is difficult work that requires a substantial commitment of time, energy, and patience from each team member.

Involving low-income and minority parents presents a particular challenge because this group of parents is often suspicious of the integrity of any school change process (Annie E. Casey Foundation, 1995). There is a history of mistrust between low-income and minority parents and schools because

---

A New Model of School Discipline

these parents have never been true partners engaged in meaningful school decisions. As a result, outreach efforts must specifically target low-income and minority parents, and efforts must be made to win over and engage them as collaborative team members.

Stage 4: Review of Best Practices at Each Systemic Level

This stage involves conducting a review of best practices to ensure that this new initiative uses scientific knowledge regarding what works at each systemic level: primary/universal, secondary/targeted, and tertiary/remedial. I have already carried out this step for changing the discipline model of a school in Chapter 4. Once a comprehensive array of programs and strategies at each intervention level has been selected for implementation, a plan for training and providing support for school staff should be discussed and decided upon. The acquisition of new skills necessary for shifting from an ingrained traditional disciplinary approach to a new disciplinary approach requires a lot of coaching in a climate of encouragement (e.g., "mistakes are learning experiences") and honest feedback and support. To do this, the following questions need to be answered: Who gets trained and in what order? Who will provide this training (does an outside training consultant need to be hired to provide this training)? What funding is required for this training? What incentives for change will be used, such as intrinsically valued outcomes, expectations for success, recognition, and rewards? What can be done to institutionalize support mechanisms to maintain and evolve changes and to generate periodic renewal of change efforts?

Stage 5: Realignment of School Policies With New Practices

This stage involves a policy review process and the realignment of school policy with new practices. For example, a new way of thinking about discipline must occur at the beginning of this process, and this new way of thinking must be integrated throughout school policies. A number of discipline policy issues that I raised in Chapter 4 need to be addressed in this process. For example, disciplinary data should clearly define student offenses as well as include specific information on disciplinary actions taken by the school and the duration of the disciplinary action. Catchall categories of offenses such as "insubordination," "disrespect," or other subjective terms should not be used in reporting disciplinary offenses. If this process does not occur, it is likely that there will be an ongoing conflict between policy and practice.

In closing, I offer several additional key points to keep in mind throughout this strategic change process:

- *Adequate funding.* "The best initiative design will contain funds that are significant enough to get the initiative going, establish legitimacy, and keep the stakeholders on board" (Annie E. Casey Foundation, 1995).
- *Small wins and "baby steps."* It is good to think big, but in reality, small wins and baby steps provide the essential foundation upon which later, larger, and lasting successes can rest. "The smaller steps must be studied in detail and the learnings of these studies widely shared and built upon" (Elias et al., 2003, p. 315).
- *Lasting organizational change can take up to 3–5 years to achieve.* This timeframe takes into account the need for key players "to balance their lives between existing efforts while they are designing and implementing new ways of doing business" (Annie E. Casey Foundation, 1995, p. 8). Some efforts at major systemic change have failed because they "suffered from the twin problems of accolades that were given too early followed by criticism and disappointment that were equally premature" (Annie E. Casey Foundation, 1995, p. 21).
- *Efforts need to be sustained over time and through changes in leadership.* It is important to take the necessary steps to sustain the effort over time and through changes in leadership (Annie E. Casey Foundation, 1995). For example, a charismatic, politically skillful leader may move on to another job and other changes in leadership may occur over time; therefore, "transition periods" or "capacity building" periods will occur and 'readiness' and 'will' need to be reassessed throughout the initiative" (Annie E. Casey Foundation, 1995, p. 13). It must be anticipated that there may be frequent turnover among project staff and rates of attrition among teachers (50% among new teachers in their first 3 years) and school superintendents (an average of 2 years) (Elias et al., 2003).

- *Significant modifications over time should not be viewed as a sign of failure.* "The best original plans for complex multiyear change will require repair, revision, reassessment, and recommitment . . . significant modification cannot be a sign of failure." (Annie E. Casey Foundation, 1995, p. 19)

Summary

A number of significant obstacles and challenges should be anticipated in making any type of organizational change in schools. Particular challenges face those who desire to change school discipline practices because the current traditional punitive model of discipline is deeply embedded in the culture and climate of the vast majority of U.S. public schools. Change is much more likely to be successful and sustained over time by developing and implementing a strategic planning process that is specifically designed to move from a traditional, punitive model of school discipline to a relationship-based model of discipline. Several additional key points are important to consider in making significant systemic changes in schools, including a recognition that small wins and "baby steps" provide the essential foundation upon which later, larger, and lasting successes can rest, and that lasting organizational change can take up to 3–5 years to achieve. It is also important to remember that efforts need to be sustained over time and through changes in leadership and that significant modifications over time should not be viewed as a sign of failure.

References

Adelman, H. S., & Taylor, L. (1997). Addressing barriers to learning: Beyond school-linked services and full service schools. *American Journal of Orthopsychiatry, 67*, 408–421.

Adelman, H. S., & Taylor, L. (2007). Systemic change for school improvement. *Journal of Educational and Psychological Consultation, 17*, 55–77.

American, Academy of Pediatrics. (2003). Out-of-school suspension and expulsion. *Committee on School Health, 112*, 1206–1209.

Annie, E. Casey Foundation. (1995). *The path of most resistance: Reflections on lessons learned from New Futures.* Baltimore: Author.

Aspy, D. N., & Roebuck, F. N. (1977). *Kids don't learn from people they don't like.* Amherst, MA: Human Resource Development Press.

Bacon, E. H. (1990). Disciplining handicapped students: Legal issues in light of *Honig v. Doe. Academic Therapy, 25*, 599–611.

Barnes, R. (2009). Student strip search illegal. *The Washington Post,* June 26, 2009. Retrieved June 25, 2009, from http://www.washingtonpost.com/wp-dyn/content/article/2009/06/25

Barrish, H. H., Saunders, M., & Wold, M. M. (1969). Good behavior game: Effects of individual contingencies for group consequences on disruptive behavior in a classroom. *Journal of Applied Behavior Analysis, 2*, 119–124.

Battistich, V., & Hom, A. (1997). The relationship between students' sense of their school as a community and their involvement in problem behaviors. *American Journal of Public Health, 87*, 1997–2001.

Bauer, G. B., Dubanoski, R., Yamanchi, L. A., & Honbo, K. A. M. (1990). Corporal punishment and the schools. *Education and Urban Society, 22*, 285–299.

Bear, G. G., Cavalier, A. R., & Manning, M. A. (2002). *Best practices in school discipline.* In A. Thomas & J. Grimes (Eds.), *Best practices in school psychology* (pp. 977–991). Bethesda, MD: National Association of School Psychologists.

Bear, G. B., & Smith, D. C. (2009). *Fact sheet #7: School climate.* Retrieved May 15, 2009, from the Consortium to Prevent School Violence Web site: http://www.preventschoolviolence.org

Beer, M., & Nohria, N. (2000). *Breaking the code of change.* Boston: Harvard Business School Press.

Belenardo, S. J. (2001). Practices and conditions that lead to a sense of community in middle schools. *NASSP Bulletin, 85,* 1–7.

Berger, J. (2008, July 16). In schools, how tight must discipline be? *New York Times.* Retrieved September, 15, 2008, from http://www.nytimes.com/2008/07/06/nyregion/nyregionspecial2/06colwe.html?pagewanted=2&sq=In%20schools,%20how%20tight%20must%20discipline%20be?&st=nyt&scp=1

Bernstein, R., & Edwards, T. (2008, August 14). An older and more diverse nation by midcentury. Retrieved September 30, 2008, from http://www.k12.wa.us/research/pubdocs/pdf/dropoutreport2003.pdf

Bloomberg, N. (2004). Effective discipline for misbehavior: In school vs. out of school suspension. Retrieved August 15, 2007 from Villanova University Web site: http://www.publications.villanova.edu/Concept/2004/Effective_Discipline.pdf

Blum, R. W., McNeely, C., & Rinehart, P. M. (2002). *Improving the odds: the untapped power of schools to improve the health of teens.* Minneapolis: Center for Adolescent Health and Development, University of Minnesota.

Bock, S., Tapscott, K. E., & Savner, J. L. (1998). Suspension and expulsion: Effective management for students? *Intervention in School and Clinic, 34,* 50–52.

Bradshaw, C. P., Koth, C. W., Thornton, L. A., & Leaf, P. J. (2009). Altering school climate through positive behavioral interventions and supports: Findings from a group-randomized trial. *Prevention Science, 10,* 100–115.

Bradshaw, C. P., Reinke, W. M., Brown, L. D., Bevans, K. B., & Leaf, P. J. (2008). Implementation of school-wide Positive Behavioral Interventions and Supports (PBIS) in elementary schools: Observations from a randomized trial. *Education & Treatment of Children, 31,* 1–26.

Brantlinger, E. (1995). Social class in school: Student' perspectives. *Research Bulletin, PhiDelta Kappa Center for Evaluation, Development and Research, 14.* Retrieved February 10, 2003, from http://www.kupdk.org/research/internatinal/resbull.14.htm.

Brooks, K., Schiraldi, V., & Ziedenberg, J. (2000). *School house hype: Two years later.* Washington, DC: Justice Policy Institute and Covington, KY: Children's Law Center, Inc.

Browne, J. A. (2003). *Derailed: The schoolhouse to jailhouse track.* Retrieved March 2, 2006, from the Advancement Project Web site: http://www.advancement-project.org

Bruns, E. J., Moore, E., Stephan, S. H., Pruitt, D., & Weist, M. D. (2005). The impact of school mental health services on out-of-school suspension rates. *Journal of Youth and Adolescence, 34,* 23–30.

Burchard, J. D. (2000). How wraparound can help overcome three common barriers to successful transition services. *Reaching Today's Youth, 2,* 49–51.

Cable, M. (1975). *The little darlings.* New York: Scribner & Sons.

CASEL. (2007a). *CASEL briefs: Background on social and emotional learning*. Retrieved March 5, 2009, from http://www.casel.org/downloads/SEL&CASELbackground. pdf

CASEL. (2007b). *The benefits of school-based social and emotional learning programs: Highlights from a forthcoming CASEL report*. Retrieved April 11, 2009, http:// www.casel.org/downloads/metaanalysissum.pdf

Cauley, K. M., & Jovanovich, D. (2006). Developing an effective transition program for students entering middle school or high school. *The Clearing House, 80*, 15–25.

Center for Mental Health Studies at UCLA. (2005). *What are the alternatives to suspension?* Retrieved March 8, 2007, from: http://smph.psych.ucla.edu/netex-change.aspx?tag=279

Center for Mental Health in Schools at UCLA. (2006). *A technical aid packet on resource mapping and management to address barriers to learning: An intervention for systemic change*. Los Angeles: Author.

Center for Mental Health Services in Schools at UCLA. (2007). *Dropout prevention*. Los Angeles: Author.

Center for Mental Health Services in Schools at UCLA. (n.d.a). *Systemic change and empirically-supported practices: The implementation problem*. Los Angeles: Author.

Center for Mental Health Services in School at UCLA. (n.d.b). *Organization facilitators: A key change agent for systemic school and community changes*. Los Angeles: Author.

Centers for Disease Control and Prevention. (2009). *School connectedness: Strategies for increasing protective factors among youth*. Atlanta, GA: US Department of Health and Human Services.

Chalmers, I. (2003). Trying to do more good than harm in policy and practice: The role of rigorous, transparent, up-to-date evaluations. *The ANNALS of the American Academy of Political and Social Science, 589*, 22–40.

Cherniss, C., & Adler, M. (2000). *Promoting emotional intelligence in organizations*. Washington, DC: American Society for Training and Development.

Civil Rights Project at Harvard University. (2000). *Opportunities suspended: The devastating consequences of zero tolerance and school discipline policies*. (Report by the Advancement Project and the Civil Rights Project). Boston: Author.

Classroom Organization and Management Program. (2004). *Creating conditions for learning*. Retrieved on May 20, 2009, from http://www.comp.org/abou-tus_research.htm#

Coalition for Juvenile Justice. (2001). *Abandoned in the back row: New lessons in education and delinquency prevention*. Retrieved September 11, 2009, from http://www.juvjustice.org/media/resources/resource_122.pdf

Comer, J. P. (2001). Schools that develop children. *The American Prospect, 12,* 30–35.

DeJong, W. (1999). *Building the peace: The Resolving Conflict Creatively Program.* Washington, DC: National Institute of Justice.

Delisio, E. (2003). *In-school suspension: A learning tool.* Retrieved March 2, 2007, from the Education World Web site: http://www.education-world.com/ a_admin/admin/admin329.shtml

Denning, S. (2005). *The leader's guide to storytelling: Mastering the art and discipline of business narrative.* Hoboken, NJ: Jossey-Bass.

Denning, S. (2007). *The secret language of leadership: How leaders inspire action through narrative.* Hoboken, NJ: Jossey-Bass.

Deridder, L. M. (1990). The impact of school suspensions and expulsions on dropping out. *Educational Horizons, 60,* 153–157.

Deutsch, M., Mitchell, V., Zhang, Q., Khattri, N., Tepavac, L., Weitzman, E. A., et al. (1992). *The effects of training in cooperative learning and conflict resolution in an alternative high school.* New York: Columbia University.

Dignity in Schools Campaign. (2008). Children are being pushed out of school. Retrieved on June 1, 2009, from http://www.dignityinschools.org/summary. php?index=158

Dinkes, R., Kemp, J., & Baum, K. (2009). *Indicators of school crime and safety: 2008* (NCES 2009-022/NCJ 226343). Washington, DC: National Center for Education Statistics and Bureau of Justice Statistics. Office of Justice Programs, U.S. Department of Justice. Washington, DC.

Dryfoos, J. G. (1994). *Full service: A revolution in health and social services for children, youth, and families.* San Francisco: Jossey-Bass.

Dupper, D. R. (2007). Incorporating best practices. In L. Bye & M. Alvarez (Eds.), *School social work: Theory to practice* (pp. 212–224). Belmont, CA: Thomson Brooks/Cole.

Dwyer, K., & Osher, D. (2000). *Safeguarding our children: An action guide.* Washington, DC: US Departments of Education and Justice, American Institutes for Research.

Dwyer, K., Osher, D., & Warger, C. (1998). *Early warning, timely response: A guide to safe schools.* Washington, DC: US Department of Education.

Eber, L., Nelson, C. M., & Miles, P. (1997). School-based wraparound for students with emotional and behavioral challenges. *Exceptional Children, 63,* 539–555.

Eckstrom, R. B., Goertz, M. E., Pollack, J. M., & Rock, D. A. (1986). Who drops out of high school and why?: Findings from a national study. *Teachers College Record, 87,* 357–73.

Education Law Center. (2007). *Student discipline.* Retrieved on April 9, 2009, from http://www.edlawcenter.org/ELCPublic/StudentRights/StudentDiscipline.htm

Elias, M. J. (2001). Middle school transition: It's harder than you think. Making the transition to middle school successful. *Middle Matters, 10,* 1–2.

Elias, M. J., Zins, J. E., Graczyk, P. A., & Weissberg, R. P. (2003). Implementation, sustainability, and scaling up of emotional and academic innovations in public schools. *School Psychology Review, 32,* 303–319.

Epstein, R. (2007, April/May). The myth of the teen brain. *Scientific American Mind.* 57-63. Retrieved on April 8, 2009, from http://www.sciam.com/article. cfm?id=the-myth-of-the-teen-brain

Epstein, M., Atkins, M., Cullinan, D., Kutash, K., & Weaver, R. (2008). *Reducing behavior problems in the elementary school classroom: A practice guide* (NCEE # 2008-012). Washington, DC: National Center for Education Evaluation and Regional Assistance.

Erchul, W. P., & Martens, B. K. (1997). *School consultation: Conceptual and empirical bases of practice.* New York: Plenum Press.

Everhart, K., & Wandersmann, A. (2000). Applying comprehensive quality programming and empowerment evaluation to reduce implementation barriers. *Journal of Educational and Psychological Consultation, 11,* 177–191.

Everson, S. T. (1995). Selecting school improvement programs. In J. H. Block, S. T. Everson, & T. R. Guskey (Eds.), *School improvement programs: A handbook for educational leaders* (pp. 433–452). New York: Scholastic.

Evertson, C. M., & Weinstein, C. S. (2006). Classroom management as a field of inquiry. In C. M. Evertson & C. S. Weinstein (Eds.), *Handbook of classroom management: Research, practice, and contemporary issues* (pp. 3–15). Mahwah, NJ: Erlbaum.

Fallona, C., & Richardson, V. (2006). Classroom management as a moral activity. In C. M. Evertson & C. S. Weinstein (Eds.), *Handbook of classroom management: Research, practice, and contemporary issues* (pp. 1041–1062). Mahwah, NJ: Erlbaum.

Family Resources. (2001). *Highlights from the evaluation of the on-campus intervention program by the Louis de la Parte Florida Mental Health Center at the University of South Florida.* Retrieved March 8, 2009, from http://www.family-resources. org/asp/programs_ocipreport01.asp

Fashola, O. S., & Slavin, R. E. (1998). Effective dropout prevention and college attendance programs for students placed at risk. *Journal of Education for Students Placed at Risk, 3,* 159–183.

Feindler, E. L., Marriot, S. A., & Iwata, M. (1984). Group anger control for junior high school delinquents. *Cognitive Therapy & Research, 8,* 299–311.

Fenning, P. A., & Bohanon, H. (2006). Schoolwide discipline policies: An analysis of discipline codes of conduct. In C. M. Evertson & C. S. Weinstein (Eds.), *Handbook of classroom management: Research, practice, and contemporary issues* (pp. 1021–1040). Mahwah, NJ: Erlbaum.

Ford, J. D., Ford, L. W., & D'Amelio, A. (2008). Resistance to change: The rest of the story. *Academy of Management Review, 33,* 362–377.

Fredricks, J. A., Blumenfeld, P. C., & Paris, A. H. (2004). School engagement: Potential of the concept, state of the evidence. *Review of Educational Research, 74*, 59–109.

Freiberg, H. J., & Lapointe, J. M. (2006). Research–based programs for preventing and solving discipline problems. In C. M. Evertson & C. S. Weinstein (Eds.), *Handbook of Classroom management: Research, practice, and contemporary issues* (pp. 735–786). Mahwah, NJ: Erlbaum.

Freiberg, H. J., & Stein, T. A. (1999). Measuring, improving and sustaining healthy learning environments. In H. J. Freiberg (Ed.), *School climate: Measuring, improving and sustaining healthy learning environments* (pp. 11–29). London: Falmer Press.

Freiberg, H. J., Stein, T. A., & Huang, S. (1995). Effects of a classroom management intervention on student achievement in inner-city elementary schools. *Educational Research and Evaluation, 1*, 36–66.

Gay, G. (2006). Connections between classroom management and culturally responsive teaching. In C. M. Evertson & C. S. Weinstein (Eds.), *Handbook of classroom management: Research, practice, and contemporary issues* (pp. 343–370). Mahwah, NJ: Erlbaum.

Gibbs, L. & Gambrill, E. (1999). *Critical thinking for social workers: Exercises for the helping professions* (2nd ed.). Thousand Oaks, CA: Pine Forge Press.

Gilley, A., Gilley, J. W., & McMillan, H. S. (2009). Organizational change: Motivation, communication, and leadership effectiveness. *Performance Improvement Quarterly, 21*, 75–94.

Global Progress. (2008). *Lawfulness of corporal punishment-United States of America*. Retrieved July 19, 2008, from http://www.endcorporalpunishment. org/pages/progress/reports/usa.html

Good Behavior Game. (n.d.) Intervention central. Retrieved May 2, 2009, from http://www.interventioncentral.org/htmdocs/interventions/classroom/gbg. php *Goss v. Lopez*, 419 U.S. 565 (1975).

Gottfredson, D. (2001). *Schools and delinquency*. Cambridge, England: Cambridge University Press.

Gottfredson, D., Gottfredson, G. D., & Hybl, L. G. (1993). Managing adolescent behavior: A multi-year, multischool study. *American Educational Research Journal, 30*, 179–215.

Government Accountability Office (2009, May). *Seclusions and restraints: Selected cases of death and abuse at public and private schools and treatment centers* (GAO - 09-719T). Washington, DC: Author.

Greenberg, M. T., Domitrovich, C., & Bumbarger, B. (2000). *Preventing mental disorders in school-age children: A review of the effectiveness of prevention programs*. University Park, PA: Pennsylvania State University, Prevention

Research Center for the Promotion of Human Development, College of Health and Human Development.

Greenberg, M. T., Weissberg, R. P., O'Brien, M. U., Zins, J. E., Fredericks, L., Resnik, H., & Elias, M. J. (2003). School-based prevention: Promoting positive social development through social and emotional learning. *American Psychologist, 58*, 466–474.

Greene, R. W. (2008). *Lost at school: Why our kids with behavioral challenges are falling through the cracks and how we can help them.* New York: Scribner.

Grossman, J. B., & Bulle, M. J. (2006). Review of what youth programs do to increase the connectedness of youth with adults. *Journal of Adolescent Health, 39*, 788–799.

Hamilton, M. L., & Richardson, V. (1995). Effects of the culture in two schools on the process and outcomes of staff development. *Elementary School Journal, 95*, 367–385.

Harris, V. W., & Sherman, J. A. (1973). Use and analysis of the "Good Behavior Game" to reduce disruptive classroom behavior. *Journal of Applied Behavior Analysis, 6*, 405–417.

Hatch, T. (2000). What does it take to break the mold? Rhetoric and reality in new American schools. *Teachers College Record, 102*, 561–589.

Hawkins, J. D., Catalano, R. F., & Miller, J. Y. (1991). Risk and protective factors for alcohol and other drug problems in adolescence and early adulthood: Implications for substance abuse prevention. *Psychological Bulletin, 112*, 64–105.

Henggeler, S. W., Schoenwald, S. K., Borduin, C. M., Rowland, M. D., & Cunningham, P. B. (1998). *Multisystemic treatment of anti-social behavior in children and adolescents.* New York: Guilford Press.

Herrera, C., Grossman, J. B., Kauh, T. J., Feldman, A. F., & McMaken, J. (2007). *Making a difference in schools: The Big Brothers Big Sisters school-based mentoring impact study.* Philadelphia: Public/Private Ventures.

Hooper-Briar, K., & Lawson, H. (1994, September). *Expanding partnerships for vulnerable children, youth, and families.* Paper presented at the meeting of the Council on Social Work Education, Alexandria, VA.

Horner, R. H., Sugai, G., Todd, A. W., & Lewis-Palmer, T. (2005). School-wide positive behavior support. In L. Bambara & L. Kern (Eds.), *Individualized supports for students with problem behaviors: Designing positive behavior plans* (pp. 359–390). New York: Guilford.

Housewright, E. (1999, October 17). Troubled children: Intervention, therapy called key for youths with mental disorders. *The Dallas Morning News*, p. 1A.

Human Rights Watch. (2008). *A violent education: Corporal punishment of children in US public schools.* New York: Author.

Hyman, I. A. (1995). Corporal punishment, psychological maltreatment, violence, and punitiveness in America: Research, advocacy, and public policy. *Applied and Preventive Psychology, 4*, 113–130.

Hyman, I. A., & Perrone, D. C. (1998). The other side of school violence: Educator policies and practices that may contribute to student misbehavior. *Journal of School Psychology, 36*, 7–27.

Indiana University. (2000a). *Early identification and intervention.* Retrieved May 5, 2009, from http://www.indiana.edu/~safeschl/early.html

Indiana University. (2000b). *Creating a positive climate: Peer mediation.* Retrieved May 10, 2009, from http://www.indiana.edu/~safeschl/PeerMediation.pdf

Indiana University. (2002a). *Effective responses: Teen courts.* Retrieved May 5, 2009, from http://www.indiana.edu/~safeschl/teen_courts.pdf

Indiana University. (2002b). *Effective Responses: Wraparound.* Retrieved May 5, 2009, from http://www.indiana.edu/~safeschl/wraparound.pdf

Indiana University. (2002c). *Building safe and responsive schools: System wide training in preventive school discipline.* Retrieved April 10, 2009, from http://www.indiana.edu/~safeschl/about.html

Ingersoll S., & LeBoeuf, D. (1997). *Reaching out to youth out of the educational mainstream.* Washington, DC: Office of Juvenile Justice and Delinquency Prevention.

Ingraham v. Wright, 430 U.S. 651, 97S. Ct. 1401 (1977).

Is school-wide positive behavior support an evidence-based practice? (2009, March). Retrieved on August 4, 2009, from http://www.pbis.org/common/pbisresources/publications/EvidenceBaseSWPBS08_04_08.doc

Jenson, J. M. (2006). Advances and challenges in preventing childhood and adolescent problem behavior. *Social Work Research, 30*, 131–134.

Johnson, B., Whitington, V., & Oswald, M. (1994). Teacher's views of school discipline: A theoretical framework. *Cambridge Journal of Education, 24*, 266–276.

Kaufman, P., Chen, X., Choy, S. P., Ruddy, S. A., Miller, A. K., Fleury, J. K., Chandler, K. A., Rand, M. R., Klaus, P., & Planty, M. G. (2000). *Indicators of school crime and safety, 2000.* U.S. Departments of Education and Justice. NCES 2001– 017/NCJ-184176. Washington, D.C.: 2000.

Kimmel, J. (n.d.). *Why do we hurt our children?* Retrieved December 12, 2007, from The Natural Child Project Web site: http://www.naturalchild.org/james_kimmel/punishment.htm

Knoff, H. M. (2002). Best practices in facilitating school reform, organizational change, and strategic planning. In A. Thomas & J. Grimes (Eds.), *Best practices in school psychology* (pp. 235–253). Bethesda, MD: National Association of School Psychologists.

Lam, J. (1989). *The impact of conflict resolution programs on schools: A review and synthesis of the evidence* (2nd ed.). Amherst: MA: National Association for Mediation in Education.

Larson, J. (1994). Violence prevention in the schools: A review of selected programs and procedures. *School Psychology Review, 23,* 151–165.

Larson, K. A. (1995). *Redefining troublemakers,* Speech at the Office of Special Education Training Conference, Washington, DC.

Libbey, H. P. (2004). Measuring student relationships to school: Attachment, bonding, connectedness, and engagement. *Journal of School Health, 74,* 274–283.

London, P. (1987). Character education and clinical intervention: A paradigm shift for US schools. *Phi Delta Kappan, 68,* p. 671

Mayer, M. J., & Leone, P. E. (2007). School violence and disruption revisited: Equity and safety in the school house. *Focus on Exceptional Children, 40,* 1–28.

McNeely, C. A., Nonnemaker, J. M., & Blum, R. W. (2002). Promoting school connectedness: Evidence from the National Longitudinal Study of Adolescent Health. *Journal of School Health, 72,* 138–146.

McPartland, J. M., & Slavin, R. E. (1990). *Increasing achievement of at-risk students at each grade level.* Washington, DC: U.S. Department of Education, Office of Educational Research and Improvement, ED 318134.

Medland, M. B., & Stachnik, T. J. (1972). Good-behavior game: A replication and systematic analysis. *Journal of Applied Behavior Analysis, 5,* 45–51.

Metz, M. H. (1983). Sources of constructive social relationships in urban magnet school. *American Journal of Education, 91,* 202–215.

Mihalic, S. F., & Grotpeter, J. K. (1997). *Blueprints for violence prevention: Book two-Big Brothers/Big Sisters of America.* Boulder, CO: Institute of Behavioral Science.

Milner, H. R. (2006). Classroom management in urban classrooms. In C. M. Evertson & C. S. Weinstein (Eds.), *Handbook of classroom management: Research, practice, and contemporary issues* (pp. 491–522). Mahwah, NJ: Erlbaum.

Moffitt, T. E. (1994). Adolescent-limited and life-course persistent antisocial behavior: A developmental taxonomy. *Psychological Review, 100,* 674–701.

Morrison, B., Blood, P., & Thorsborne, M. (2005). Practicing restorative justice in school communities: The challenge of culture change. *Public Organization Review: A Global Journal, 5,* 335–357.

Morrison, G. M., & Skiba, R. (2001). Promises and perils. *Psychology in the Schools, 38,* 173–184.

Moshman, D. (1999). *Adolescent psychological development: Rationality, morality, and identity.* Mahwah, NJ: Erlbaum.

MST Services. (2007). *MST service: Research on effectiveness.* Retrieved on May 2, 2009, from http://www.mstservices.com/research_on_effectiveness.php

---

MST Services. (n.d.). *Multisystemic therapy: Clinical outcomes and cost savings.* Retrieved on May 2, 2009, from http://www.mstservices.com/outcomes_1a.pdf

National Education Association. (2005). *C.A.R.E.: Strategies for closing the achievement gaps- NEA guide for educators.* Retrieved March 5, 2007, from http://www.nea.org/teachexperience/careguide.html

New Jersey v. T.L.O., 469 U.S. 325 (1985).

Noguera, P. A. (2001). Finding safety where we least expect it: The role of social capital in preventing school violence. In W. Ayers, B. Dohrn, & R. Ayers (Eds.), *Zero tolerance: Resisting the drive for punishment in our schools* (pp. 202–218). New York: New Press.

Northeast Foundation for Children Inc (n.d.). *Responsive classroom: Creating safe, challenging, and joyful elementary classrooms and schools.* Retrieved on May 19, 2009, from http://www.responsiveclassroom.org/about/research.html.

Ohio Commission on Dispute Resolution and Conflict Management. (1994). *Conflict management in schools: Sowing seeds for a safer society.* Columbus, OH: Author.

Olweus, D. (1993). *Bullying at school: What we know and what we can do.* Oxford, England: Blackwell.

Ozer, E. (2005). The impact of violence on urban adolescents: Longitudinal effects of perceived school connection and family support. *Journal of Adolescent Research, 20,* 167–192.

Parker-Pope, T. (2008, September 15). *It's not discipline, it's a teachable moment.* New York Times. Retrieved March 10, 2009, from http://www.nytimes.com/2008/09/15/health/healthspecial2/15discipline.html.

Payne, A. A., Gottfredson, D. C., & Gottfredson, G. D. (2006). School predictors of the intensity of implementation of school-based prevention programs. *Prevention Science, 7,* 225–237.

Payton, J., Weissberg, R. P., Durlak, J. A., Dymnicki, A. B., Taylor, R. D., Schellinger, K. B., & Pachan, M. (2008). *The positive impact of social and emotional learning for kindergarten to eighth-grade students: Findings from three scientific reviews.* Chicago: Collaborative for Academic, Social, and Emotional Learning.

Peterson, R. L. (2008). *Fact sheet #6: Student uniforms.* Retrieved April 20, 2009, from the Consortium to Prevent School Violence Web site: http://www.preventschoolviolence.org.

Peterson, S. B., & Beres, J. (2008). *Report to the nation: The global youth justice movement, 15 year update on youth courts and teen courts.* Highland Hills, OH: Global Issues Resource Center.

Pilarski, M. (1994). Student teachers: Underprepared for classroom management? *Teaching Education, 6,* 77–80.

Porter, A. J. (2007). *Restorative practices in schools: Research reveals power of restorative approach, Part I.* Retrieved on April 10, 2009, from the International Institute for Restorative Practices Web site: http://www.iirp.org

Quindlen, A. (1999, November 11). Mentally ill kids exist on margins. *Denver Rocky Mountain News*, p. 35A.

Raffaele Mendez, L. M., & Knoff, H. M. (2003). Who gets suspended from school and why: A demographic analysis of schools and disciplinary infractions in a large school district. *Education and Treatment of Children, 26*, 30–51.

Raffaele Mendez, L. M. (2003). Predictors of suspension and negative school outcomes: A longitudinal investigation. In J. Wald & D. L. Losen (Eds.), *New directions for youth development* (no. 99: Deconstructing the school-to-prison pipeline). (pp. 17–34). San Francisco: Jossey-Bass.

Raines, J. C. (2008). *Evidence based practice in school mental health.* New York: Oxford University Press.

Rathvon, N. (1999). *Effective school interventions: Strategies for enhancing academic achievement and social competence.* New York: The Guilford Press.

Rausch, M. K., & Skiba, R. J. (2004). *Unplanned outcomes: Suspensions and expulsions in Indiana.* Retrieved January 10, 2007, from the Center for Evaluation and Education Policy Web site: http://ceep.indiana.edu/ChildrenLeftBehind

Rausch, M. K., & Skiba, R. (2006). *Discipline, disability, and race: Disproportionality in Indiana schools.* Education Policy Brief, Center for Evaluation and Education Policy, Vol. 4 (10). Retrieved January 10, 2007 from http://www.ceep.indiana.edu/pub.shtml#ed

Reid, J. B. (1993). Prevention of conduct disorder before and after school entry: Relating interventions to developmental findings. *Development and Psychopathology, 5*, 243–262.

Richart, D., Brooks, K., & Soler, M. (2003, February). *Unintended consequences: The impact of "zero tolerance" and other exclusionary policies on Kentucky students.* Retrieved March 18, 2006, from the Building Blocks for Youth Web site: http://www.buildingblocksforyouth.org

Riordan, G. (2006). Reducing student 'suspension rates' and engaging students in learning: Principal and teacher approaches that work. *Improving Schools, 9*, 239–250.

Rossow, L. F., & Parkinson, J. (1999). *The law of student expulsions and suspensions.* Dayton, OH: Education Law Association.

Ryan, A. M., & Patrick, H. (2001). The classroom social environment and changes in adolescents' motivation and engagement during middle school. *American Educational Research Journal, 38*, 437–460.

Safford Unified School District #1 v. Redding, No. 08-479, 531 F.3d 1071 June 25, 2009.

Safran, S., & Safran, J. (1985). Classroom context and teachers' perceptions of problem behaviors. *Journal of Educational Psychology, 77*, 20–28

Samuels, C. A. (2009, March 4). 'What Works' guide weighs in on RTI. *Education Week*. Retrieved June 3, 2009, from the Education week web site: http://www.edweek.org/ew/articles/2009/03/02/23rti.h28.html & destination/

Sanders, D. (2001). A caring alternative to suspension. *Education Digest, 66*, 51–54.

Sarason, S. B. (1990). *The predictable failure of educational reform: Can we change before it's too late?* San Francisco: Jossey-Bass.

Schimmel, D. (2006). Classroom management, discipline, and the law: Clarifying confusions about students' rights and teachers' authority. In C. M. Evertson & C. S. Weinstein (Eds.), *Handbook of classroom management: Research, practice, and contemporary issues* (pp. 1005–1019). Mahwah, NJ: Erlbaum.

Schinke, S. P., & Gilchrist, L. D. (1984). *Life skills counseling with adolescents*. Baltimore: University Park Press.

Schlegel, A., & Barry, H. III. (1991). *Adolescence: An anthropological inquiry*. New York: Free Press.

Schoenwald, S. K., Henggeler, S. W., Brondino, M. J., & Rowland, M.D. (2000). Multisystemic therapy: Monitoring treatment fidelity. *Family Process, 39*, 83–103.

Scott, T. M., & Barrett, S. B. (2004). Using staff and student time engaged in disciplinary procedures to evaluate the impact of school-wide PBS. *Journal of Positive Behavior Interventions, 6*, 21–27.

Skager, R. (2007). *Effective and humane youth policy starts by treating youth with respect*. Retrieved March 28, 2009, from the International Institute for Restorative Practices Web site: http://www.iirp.org

Skiba, R. J. (2000). *Zero tolerance, zero evidence: An analysis of school disciplinary practices* (Policy Research Report No. SRS2). Bloomington, IN: Indiana Education Policy Center.

Skiba, R., Boone, K., Fontanini, A., Wu, T., Strussell, A., & Peterson, R. (n.d.). *Preventing school violence: A practical guide to comprehensive planning*. Bloomington, IN: The Safe and Responsive Schools Project at the Indiana Education Policy Center.

Skiba, R. J., Michael, R. S., Nardo, A. C., & Peterson, R. (2002). *The color of discipline: Sources of racial and gender disproportionality in school punishment* (Policy Research Report No. SRS1). Bloomington, IN: Indiana Education Policy Center.

Skiba, R., & Peterson, R. (2000). The dark side of zero tolerance: Can punishment lead to safe schools? *Phi Delta Kappan, 80*, 372–376, 381–382.

Skiba, R. J., Peterson, R. L., & Williams, T. (1997). Office referrals and suspension: Disciplinary intervention in middle schools. *Education and Treatment of Children, 20*, 295–315.

Skiba, R., & Rausch, M. (2006). Zero tolerance, suspension, and expulsion: Questions of equity and effectiveness. In C. M. Evertson & C. S. Weinstein

(Eds.), *Handbook of classroom management: Research, practice, and contemporary issues* (pp. 1063– 1089). Mahwah, NJ: Erlbaum.

Skiba, R., Reynolds, C. R., Graham, S., Sheras, P., Conoley, J. C., & Garcia-Vazquez, E. (2006). *Are zero tolerance policies effective in the schools? An evidentiary review and recommendations*. A Report by the American Psychological Association Zero Tolerance Task Force. Retrieved April 10, 2008 from http://www.apa.org/results.html?cx=004712435678442832158%3Auo23vzm3_zo&cof=FORID%3A11&q=zero+tolerance+task+force&sa.x=0&sa.y=0&sa=search#962

Skiba, R., Ritter, S., Simmons, A., Peterson, R., & Miller, C. (2006). The Safe and Responsive Schools Project: A school reform model for implementing best practices in violence prevention. In S. R. Jimerson & M. J. Furlong (Eds.), *The handbook of school violence and school safety* (pp. 631–650). Mahwah, NJ: Erlbaum.

Slee, R. (1999). Theorizing discipline-practical research implications for schools. In H. J. Freiberg (Ed.), *Beyond behaviorism: Changing the classroom management paradigm* (pp. 21–42). Boston: Allyn & Bacon.

Smith, D. C. (2008). *Fact sheet #4: Anger management in schools*. Retrieved May 15, 2009, from the Consortium to Prevent School Violence Web site http://www.preventschoolviolence.org

Snyder, T. D., Dillow, S. A., & Hoffman, C. M. (2007). *Digest of education statistics 2006* (NCES 2007-017). Washington, DC: US Government Printing Office.

Snyder, T. D., Dillow, S. A., & Hoffman, C. M. (2009). *Digest of education statistics 2008* (NCES 2009-020). National Center for Education Statistics, Institute of Education Sciences, U.S. Department of Education. Washington, DC.

Society for Adolescent Medicine. (2003). Corporal punishment in schools: A position paper of the Society for adolescent medicine. *Journal of Adolescent Health, 32*, 385–393.

The Sourcebook of Drug and Violence Prevention Programs for Children and Adolescents (2008). *School Transitional Environmental Program*. Violence Institute of New Jersey at UMDNJ. Retrieved April 29, 2009, from http://vinst.umdnj.edu/sdfs/Abstract.asp?Code=STEP

Sprague, J. (2008, May). *Positive behavior support implementation in Norway*. Paper presented at the Society for Prevention Research, San Francisco, CA.

Sprague, J., & Walker, H. (2000). Early identification and interventions for youth with antisocial and violent behavior. *Exceptional Children, 66*, 367–379.

Stearns, E., & Glennie, E. J. (2006). When and why dropouts leave high school. *Youth & Society, 38*, 29–57.

Stewart, E. A. (2003). School social bonds, school climate, and school misbehavior: A multilevel analysis. *Justice Quarterly, 20*, 575–604.

Sugai, G., & Horner, R. H. (1999). Discipline and behavioral support: Preferred processes and practices. *Effective School Practices, 17*, 10–22.

Sughrue, J. A. (2003). Zero tolerance for children: Two wrongs do not make a right. *Educational Administration Quarterly, 39*, 238–258.

Sullivan, E., & Keeney, E. (2008). *Teachers talk: School culture, safety, and human rights.* New York: National Economic and Social Rights Initiative (NESRI) and Teachers Unite.

School Mental Health Project (n.d.) *Supporting successful transition to ninth grade.* Retrieved on May 21, 2009 from http://smhp.psych.ucla.edu/pdfdocs/practi-cenotes/transitionsninthgrade.pdf

Taylor-Greene, S., Brown, D., Nelson, L., Longton, J., Gassman, T., Cohen, J., et al. (1997). School-wide behavioral support: Starting the year off right. *Journal of Behavioral Education, 7*, 99–112.

Teicher, S. A. (2005, March 17). To paddle or not to paddle? It's still not clear in U.S. schools. *Christian Science Monitor.* Retrieved on March 19, 2008 from http://www.csmonitor.com/2005/0317/p01s04-legn.html

Tennessee Code, Title 39, Chapter 17, Part 13, 39-17-1309

Theriot M. T., & Dupper, D. R. (in press). Student discipline problems and the transition from elementary to middle school. *Education and Urban Society.*

Tinker v. DesMoines Independent Community School, 393 U.S. 503 (1969).

Townsend, B. L. (2000). The disproportionate discipline of African American learners: Reducing school suspensions and expulsions. *Exceptional Children, 66*, 381–391.

Townsend, B. L. (2000). The disproportionate discipline of African American learners: Reducing school suspensions and expulsions. *Exceptional Children, 66*, 381–391.

US Department of Education. (2001). *Dropout rates in the United States: 2000.* (NCES Publication No. 2002-114). Washington, DC: National Center for Education Statistics.

US Department of Education, National Center for Education Statistics. (2006). *The condition of education 2006* (NCES 2006-071). Washington, DC: U.S. Government Printing Office.

Valenzuela, A. (1999). *Subtractive schooling: U.S.- Mexican youth and the politics of caring.* Albany, NY: Suny Press.

Vavrus, F., & Cole, K. (2002). "I didn't do nothin'": The discursive construction of school suspension. *The Urban Review, 34*, 87–111.

Wald, J., & Casella, R. (2006). A Battle Each Day: Teachers Talk about Discipline, Suspensions, and Zero Tolerance Policy. In A. Reyes (Ed.), *Discipline, achieve-ment, and race: Is zero tolerance the answer?* (pp. 89–104).

Wald, J., & Losen, D. J. (2003). Defining and redirecting a school-to-prison pipeline. In J. Wald & D. J. Losen (Eds.), *New directions for youth development* (no. 99: Deconstructing the school to prison pipeline) (pp. 9–15). San Francisco: Jossey-Bass.

Walker, H. M., Horner, R. H., Sugai, G., Bullis, M., Sprague, J. R., Bricker, D., & Kaufman, M. J. (1995). Integrated approaches to preventing antisocial behavior patterns among school-age children and youth. *Journal of Emotional and Behavioral Disorders, 4*, 194–209.

Walker, H. M., & Severson, H. H. (1992). *Systematic screening for behavior disorders (SSBD): User's guide and administration manual* (2nd ed.). Longmont, CA: Sopris West.

Wallace, J. M. Jr., Goodkind, S., Wallace, C. M., & Bachman, J. G. (2008). Racial, ethnic, and gender differences in school discipline among U.S. high school students: 1991-2005. *The Negro Educational Review, 59*, 47–62.

Watson, M., & Battistich, V. (2006). Building and sustaining caring communities. In C. M. Evertson & C. S. Weinstein (Eds.), *Handbook of classroom management: Research, practice, and contemporary issues* (pp. 253–279). Mahwah, NJ: Erlbaum.

Weinstein, C. S., Curran, M., & Tomlinson-Clarke, S. (2003). Culturally responsive classroom management: Awareness into action. *Theory Into Practice, 42*, 269–276.

Wilson, D. (2004). The interface of school climate and school connectedness and relationships with aggression and victimization. *Journal of School Health, 74*, 293–299.

Wishy, B. (1968). *The child and the republic*. Philadelphia: University of Pennsylvania.

Woolfolk Hoy, A., & Weinstein, C. S. (2006). Student and teacher perspectives on classroom management. In C. M. Evertson & C. S. Weinstein (Eds.), *Handbook of classroom management: Research, practice, and contemporary issues* (pp. 181–219). Mahwah, NJ: Erlbaum.

Yell, M. L., & Rozalski, M. E. (2008). The impact of legislation and litigation on discipline and student behavior in the classroom. *Preventing School Failure, 52*, 7–16.

Index

Note: Page numbers in italic type refer to terms occurring in boxes.